COURAGE
WINNING LIFE'S TOUGHEST BATTLES

MAJORING IN MEN™
The Curriculum for Men

Edwin Louis Cole

watercolor books®
Southlake, Texas

Cover design by Mick Thurber

Second printing
ISBN 1931682-15-1

Ed Cole® Library
P.O. Box 92921
Southlake, TX 76092

www.EdColeLibrary.org

Published by Watercolor Books®
P. O. Box 93234
Southlake, TX 76092
www.watercolorbooks.com

TABLE OF CONTENTS

INTRODUCTION

Welcome aboard! I am delighted to extend greetings on behalf of men from Cincinnati to Singapore, and from New York to Nepal, who are stepping up to the challenge of MAJORING IN MEN™.

My prayer, as you work through this book, is for God to reveal Himself and *yourself*, pinpointing areas of your life for change and encouraging you in your strengths, convictions and dreams.

Some men will skim through and receive some help. Others—and I trust this means you—will read the books, meditate on the truths and memorize the principles, all with the ambition of becoming great men of courage, mighty men of valor—the heroes desperately needed in today's world.

My goal is for you to be changed, educated and, most of all, deepened in conviction and revelation that comes only from drawing close to God. My dream in preparing this course is for men to rise up throughout the world to study further, teach better and reach more men than I have. To that end and for that purpose, I have devoted my life and labor for the last fifty years.

This may well be one of the most life-changing experiences of your life. Let it be. Better yet—*make it be*. Truth is like soap. It works only if it's applied.

I admire you for taking this step.

Statement of Ministry

"I have been called to speak with a prophetic voice to the men of this generation and commissioned with a ministry majoring in men to declare a standard for manhood, and that standard is 'manhood and Christlikeness are synonymous.'"

Edwin Louis Cole

"Rules of the Road"
for MAJORING IN MEN™ Curriculum

1. **Give it your all!** This curriculum is a private meeting between your heart and God's. What you put into it determines what you'll get out of it. Give God the opportunity to build character, instill dreams and visions and change your life!

2. **Buy the corresponding book** from your local bookstore. If you cannot find the book locally, you may write to Watercolor Books® at P.O. Box 93234, Southlake, TX 76092, USA, or to order with a credit card by email, log onto www.EdColeLibrary.org.

3. **Take the Self Test** after completing each lesson, using your book as needed. At the end of the book, take the Final Exam.

4. Many churches use **MAJORING IN MEN**™ curriculum and collect the Final Exams to "graduate" their students. Contact www.EdColeLibrary.org for a list of ministries that commission men.

5. **Let's get going!**

Lesson 1
Introduction: The Pattern for Ministry

Lesson 1

Introduction: The Pattern for Ministry

A. The pattern for ministry

Fill in the blanks from the "pattern for ministry," then look up and write out the verses noted.

1. _Sanctify_ yourself. *(page 7)*

    Romans 6:19 _____

    _____

    _____

    John 17:17-19 _____

    _____

    _____

2. _____ the Word. *(page 7)*

    2 Timothy 4:2 _____

    _____

    _____

3. Go _____ nothing. *(page 7)*

    Acts 11:12 _____

    _____

    _____

4. Use the _____, but don't touch the _____. *(page 7)*

    Philippians 4:15 _____

    _____

    _____

    Acts 12:23 _____

    _____

    _____

5. _____ this prayer. *(page 8)*

    Acts 4:29 _____

    _____

    _____

B. Young men need to be reached.

    1. Men need to reach young men in their teens and early twenties with the truth that _____

       _____. *(page 9)*

    2. In the Jewish tradition, a young man is considered a man at what age? *(page 9)* _____

    3. Pornographers have adopted a philosophy to get a _____ hooked. *(page 9)*

    4. Look up and read out loud Proverbs 22:6.

C. Treat young men as men!

    1. What are young men in your church or fellowship called? _____ *(page 10)*

    2. What do you call them when they enter college? _____ *(page 10)*

    3. If young men are not called "men," they will not see themselves as men with the corresponding responsibility. *(page 10)*

      ___ True   ___ False

Practical:

    1. Look up "sanctify" in a dictionary and write out the definition.

    _____

    _____

What does it mean to you?

_____

_____

2. If you are a young man, what is "training" you? _____

_____

If you are a parent of a young man, who or what is training your son? _____

_____

3. **In your own words,** how can your church or fellowship help young men recognize their manhood at an early age?

_____

_____

_____

Repeat this prayer out loud:

Father, in Jesus' Name, help me understand how to be a better man for You, both for others and for my children. Help me accept responsibility and teach others responsibility as well. And create in me a godly character that is an honor to You. Amen.

Principles I want to memorize:

Self Test   *Lesson 1*

1. The pattern for ministry includes:

   a. _____ yourself.

   b. Preach the _____.

   c. _____ doubting nothing.

   d. Use the _____ but don't touch the _____.

   e. Pray this _____ .

2. In the Jewish tradition, a man is considered a man at age _____.

3. **In your own words,** write out a definition of godly character.

   _____

   _____

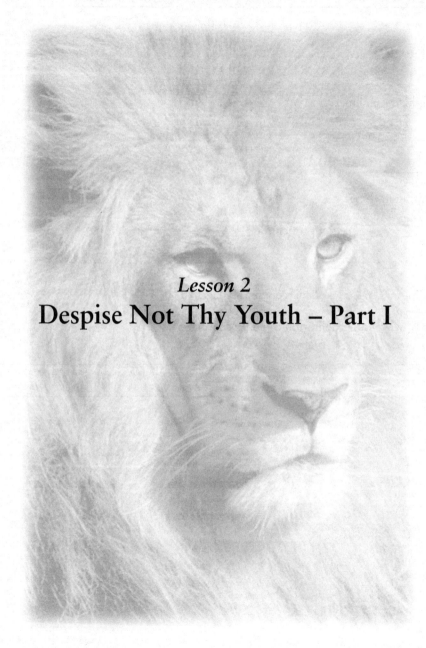

Lesson 2
Despise Not Thy Youth – Part I

Lesson 2
Despise Not Thy Youth – Part I

A. The strength of youth is its _____. *(page 13)*

    1. Read out loud: *"The glory of young men is their strength; of old men, their experience"* Proverbs 20:29 TLB.

    2. Look up and write out 1 Timothy 4:12.

    _____

    _____

    _____

B. Look up Scripture references for these great men of Scripture who were young when God dealt with them.

    1. Joseph was seventeen years old when he had his dream from God.
        Look up Genesis 37:2, 5.

    2. David was a teenager when he faced Goliath.
        Look up 1 Samuel 17:33.

For Further Study
Don't waste your youth – *"Young men likewise exhort to be sober minded"* Titus 2:6.
Recognize that, despite your youth, you are still a man – *"'O Lord God,' I said, 'I can't do that! I'm far too young! I'm only a youth!' 'Don't say that,' he replied, 'for you will go wherever I send you and speak whatever I tell you to. And don't be afraid of the people, for I, the Lord, will be with you and see you through'"* Jeremiah 1:6-8 TLB.

3.   Daniel and his three friends were young when they made their stand for God against the Babylonian king. Look up Daniel 3:17-18 and Daniel 6.

4.   Jesus was only twelve when He was reported to be teaching in the temple. Look up Luke 2:42-47.

C.   What should a young man do with his youth? *(circle all that apply) (page 14)*

1.   be ashamed of it
2.   acknowledge it
3.   channel it
4.   abuse it

D.   Here are three advantages of youth. Name three more. *(page 14)*

1.   quick ability to learn
2.   ready molding of character
3.   physical energy

4.   _____

5.   _____

6.   _____

For Further Study

Recognize the advantages of being young:
    Ability to learn quickly – 1 John 2:13
    Ready molding of character – *"It is good for a man that he bear the yoke in his youth"* Lamentations 3:27.
    Strength – Proverbs 20:29
Never be ashamed of your youth – 1 Timothy 4:12.
Acknowledge your youth, turn it toward God and revel in it – Ecclesiastes 11:9.
Realize and capitalize on the advantages of your youth – Proverbs 19:20.

E. In your opinion, what problems would a "Me-Generation" generate? *(page 16)*

_____

_____

F. Today's society has produced an image of fathers, marriages and heroes to destroy God's pattern for each. Name three poor images that may have affected you. *(pages 16-18)*

1. _____

2. _____

3. _____

G. Men are to function in two roles as God directs them. *(page 18)*

1. _____

2. _____

3. Prophets minister from the _____ to the _____.

4. Priests minister from the _____ to the _____.

For Further Study

Destructive forces facing youth today:

    The "Me Generation" philosophy – 2 Timothy 3:1-4

    False doctrine – 1 Timothy 4:1

    The anti-hero syndrome – Proverbs 17:15

    Weakening of the father role model – 2 Timothy 3:2

Prophets emphasize the specific Word God has given them – *"The lion hath roared, who will not fear? the Lord God hath spoken, who can but prophesy?"* Amos 3:8.

Pastors balance the truth of the prophet with the total life of the congregation – 1 Peter 5:1, 2.

H. There is a difference between being a _____ and being a _____. *(page 19)*

I. Young men need the _____ of the Word, not mush. *(page 21)*

Read Hebrews 5:13-14.

What do infants live on? _____   What do adults eat? _____

Practical:

1. Regarding you as a young man, or your child if you're a grown man, name some areas of life that are strengths which you may have regarded as weaknesses.

    _____

2. What TV programs can you identify which picture fathers and marriages as ludicrous or inept and which could easily be avoided?

    _____   _____

Repeat this prayer out loud:
Father, in Jesus' Name, I desire to be used of You. I will no longer feel less of myself (or my children or others) because of age. I will start today to be the man and role model You've made me to be. I will set aside childish things and carry out Your will in my (children's) generation. Thank You for strengthening me and enabling me. I will go forth in the strength of Your Name. Amen.

For Further Study

Weakness in some church leadership: Being a "lid" – Jeremiah 6:13-14; Placating and pleasure-seeking youth pastors – Isaiah 56:10-12; Elders who create cynicism and give undue criticism to young people – Ezekiel 34:4, 5
Youth pastors give young men the meat of the Word of God and discipline them – 1 Timothy 4:11, 13.

Self Test   *Lesson 2*

1. The _____ of youth is its glory.

2. Match these Bible men whom God began using when they were young:

   ___ Jesus   a.   at 17 received his dream from God

   ___ David   b.   was 12 when He taught at the temple

   ___ Daniel   c.   faced a giant as a teenager

   ___ Joseph   d.   with three young friends made a stand for God

3. Images of poor fathers and mock marriages are dangerous to young men.

   ___ True   ___ False

4. What is the difference between a prophet and priest?

   _____

   _____

Lesson 3
Despise Not Thy Youth – Part II

Lesson 3
Despise Not Thy Youth – Part II

A. The "great commission" is to do as Jesus did and make _____. *(choose one) (page 21)*

converts   disciples   people appreciate you

B. To "train by example" is another way of saying _____. *(page 21)*

Read: *"Don't let anyone think little of you because you are young. Be their ideal; let them follow the way you teach and live; be a pattern for them in your love, your faith, and your clean thoughts"* 1 Timothy 4:12 TLB.

C. Can a young man's life be a pattern even for an older man?   ___ Yes   ___ No

Read: *"You must teach what is in accord with sound doctrine. Teach the older men to be temperate, worthy of respect, self-controlled, and sound in faith, in love and in endurance Similarly, encourage the young men to be self-controlled. In everything set them an example by doing what is good"* Titus 2:1-2; 6-7 NIV.

For Further Study
God has given us power to overcome any obstacle, enemy or attack through the truth of the patterns and principles in His Word – *"Is not my word like as a fire? saith the Lord; and like a hammer that breaketh the rock in pieces?"* Jeremiah 23:29; *"For no word from God shall be void of power"* Luke 1:37 ASV.
It is God's desire for His Church to know His patterns and principles – *"The secret things belong unto the Lord our God: but those things which are revealed belong unto us and to our children for ever, that we may do all the words of this law"* Deuteronomy 29:29.
As disciples, it is our right to know the truth – *"If ye continue in my word, then are ye my disciples indeed; And ye shall know the truth, and the truth shall make you free"* John 8:31, 32.

D. What is the "Saul Syndrome"? *(pages 21)*

_____

_____

According to Scripture, what helped cause it? *(page 21)*

_____

Read: *"And the women answered one another as they played, and said, Saul hath slain his thousands, and David his ten thousands. And Saul was very wroth, and the saying displeased him; and he said, They have ascribed unto David ten thousands, and to me they have ascribed but thousands: and what can he have more but the kingdom? And Saul eyed David from that day and forward"* 1 Samuel 18:7-9.

E. Contrast the relationship of Saul and David with that of Paul and Timothy. *(pages 21-22)*

What was different?

_____

_____

Paul saw Timothy's potential and endeavored to teach, train and disciple him. *(page 22)*

___ True   ___ False

For Further Study

Older men must resist the Saul syndrome – 1 Samuel 18:8.
Young associates and younger men are to receive the benefits of the older men's experience – Proverbs 1:8, 9; 15:5, 14; 2 Samuel 15:1-6.
Paul-Timothy discipleship: Senior pastors and older men must take time to disciple young associates and younger men – *"Now also when I am old and greyheaded, O God, forsake me not; until I have shewed thy strength unto this generation, and thy power to every one that is to come"* Psalm 71:18.

F. The characteristics of a _____ emanate from the character of the _____. *(page 22)*

    1. The characteristics of a congregation emanate from the character of the _____. *(page 22)*

    2. _____ begets _____. *(page 22)*

G. What are the five steps of the pattern in the parable of the prodigal son? *(page 24)*

    1. _____

    2. _____

    3. _____

    4. _____

    5. _____

For Further Study

The characteristics of the kingdom emanate from the character of the king – Hosea 4:9.

A pastor who loves truth will produce a congregation that loves truth – 1 Thessalonians 1:6, 7.

The pattern of the parable of the prodigal:

Rebellion: Sin never cares about anything except gratifying its own desires, heedless of the consequences – Luke 15:12.

Ruin: The prodigal began his ruin with the words "Give me" – Luke 15:13, 14.

Repentance: The pivotal point between ruin and reconciliation is characterized by the words "Make me" – "*And when he came to himself, he said,…I will arise and go to my father, and will say unto him, Father, I have sinned against heaven, and before thee, And am no more worthy to be called thy son: make me as one of thy hired servants*" Luke 15:17, 19.

Reconciliation: The prodigal returns home to his father – Luke 15:20.

Restoration: The father accepts the son and restores him to his rightful position – Luke 15:22-24.

H. Read Luke 15:11-32.

1. The pivotal point between ruin and reconciliation is _____. *(page 24)*

2. The prodigal began his destruction with two words: _____. *(page 25)*

3. The prodigal began a new life with two words: _____. *(page 25)*

I. When a person says "Make me," it shows: *(page 25)*

1. _____ to authority

2. _____ to change

3. _____ of personal responsibility

4. The beginning of _____

For Further Study

Recommitment: Words of confession and contrition reveal an attitude of repentance and obedience – *"Create in me a new, clean heart, O God, filled with clean thoughts and right desires...make me willing to obey you"* Psalm 51:3, 4, 10, 12 TLB.

Practical:

1. If you're going to be a victorious man of God, what kind of church should you be in?

    _____

    _____

2. The prodigal son was a perfect example of "the high cost of low living."

    When have you paid a price for "low living"?

    _____

    Are you now paying for bad decisions or poor character? If so, how?

    _____

    What can you do to change it?

    _____

3. Name some Bible figures you know of who paid a high price for low living.

_____

_____

Repeat this prayer out loud:

Father, in Jesus' Name, help me understand my need for discipleship. Help me get in the position to disciple as Christ discipled so I can fulfill His "great commission." I reject the "Saul Syndrome" and ask You, Father, to search my heart and show me where I am jealous of others with gifts, talents and anointings that I want for myself. I accept the anointing and ministry You have for me and set my course to walk in it without thought of competition with others. Amen.

Principles I want to memorize:

Self Test *Lesson 3*

1. A young man's life can be a pattern even for an older man.   ___ True   ___ False

2. **In your own words**, write a brief summary of the "Saul Syndrome" that occurred in Scripture and how it is still relevant today.

   _____

   _____

   _____

3. The _____ of a kingdom emanate from the _____ of the king.

4. What is the pivotal point between ruin and reconciliation?

   _____

5. What two words started the destruction of the prodigal son?

   _____

6. What two words started the prodigal's recovery?

   _____

Lesson 4
Courage

Lesson 4
Courage

A. Beware of the "church-wise."

1. The church-wise are: Self-_righteous_, self-_justified_, hardened of _heart_, deceived in their _way_. *(page 27)*

2. Projecting personality, polished in their performance, going through the motions of their religion, another term for these people is _churchwise_. *(page 29)*

3. Read: *"Do not be misled: Bad company corrupts good character"* 1 Corinthians 15:33 NIV. According to this verse, what action should you take if you are around church-wise people? *(page 29)*

   get away from them.

B. It takes courage to resist the _peer pressure_ of your friends. *(page 30)*

For Further Study
Avoid associations with the insincere "church-wise."
The church-wise show no courage – *"The wicked flee when no man pursueth: but the righteous are bold as a lion"* Proverbs 28:1.
They play religious games. Their deception is dangerous to your dedication – *"They will go to church, yes, but they won't really believe anything they hear. Don't be taken in by people like that"* 2 Timothy 3:5 TLB.

It takes courage to: *(page 30)*

1. face _reality_
2. _admit_ need
3. _change_
4. make _decisions_
5. _hold_ convictions

C. Success is not based on the ability to say "_yes_" but on the ability to say "_no_." *(page 30)*

   1. Courage can be the virtue of the _wise_ or the vanity of _fools_. *(page 30)*

   2. Paul commanded Timothy to "_flee_ youthful lusts" 2 Timothy 2:22. *(page 32)*

D. Moral cowardice is the ruin of _manhood_. *(page 32)*

   1. Double-minded men waiver between _right_ and _wrong_. *(page 32)*

   2. Because they are undecided, they are constantly _tempted_ to yield to evil. *(page 32)*

   Read: "A double minded man is unstable in _all_ his ways" James 1:8.

For Further Study

It takes courage to face reality – "Behold, thou desirest truth in the inward parts" Psalm 51:6. It takes courage to change – "And when Asa heard these words, and the prophecy of Obed the prophet, he took courage, and put away the abominable idols out of all the land...and renewed the altar of the Lord" 2 Chronicles 15:8. It takes courage to admit fault – Proverbs 28:13. It takes courage to make decisions – "Choose you this day whom ye will serve...but as for me and my house, we will serve the Lord" Joshua 24:15. It takes courage to hold convictions – "Peter and John answered and said...For we cannot but speak the things which we have seen and heard" Acts 4:18-20. It takes courage to resist peer pressure and dare to be different – Psalm 119:51, 52; Daniel 1:8. It takes courage to submit to righteousness – Psalm 119:30. It takes courage to say "no" – "I have refrained my feet from every evil way, that I might keep thy word" Psalm 119:101. It takes courage to admit a desire to be a man of God – "Depart from me, ye evildoers: for I will keep the commandments of my God" Psalm 119:115; "Choosing rather to suffer affliction with the people of God, than to enjoy the pleasures of sin for a season" Hebrews 11:25.

E. Look up in your Bible and MATCH the following courageous men with their references:

1. John the Baptist when he rebuked the king   _2_ 1 Samuel 17:45-47

2. David when he stood before Goliath   _3_ Daniel 1:8

3. Daniel in his decision not to eat the king's food   _1_ Mark 6:18

F. When you keep quiet before ungodly men, you give ___*them*___ the advantage. *(page 35)*

When you speak up for Jesus, you give yourself and ___*God*___ the advantage. *(page 35)*

1. Look up Proverbs 28:1. (Bible versions vary). *"The* ___*wicked*___ *flee when no man pursueth: but the* ___*honest*___ *are bold as a lion."*

2. Satan is the great ___*counterfeit*___ who twists God's ___*patterns*___ to achieve ___*his own perverted*___ aims. *(page 37)*

For Further Study

Knowledge: You must know right from wrong to know what to resist or accept – Psalm 119:104.

It takes courage to stand your ground, courage coupled with wisdom to know when to run – Psalm 16:8; 1 Timothy 6:11; Genesis 39:12. Courage can be the virtue of the wise or the vanity of fools – Proverbs 14:16.

Moral cowardice: Causes men to shrink from duty and danger, to dread pain and to yield to fear – 1 Samuel 15:24. The fear of man is a form of moral cowardice – Proverbs 29:25. Moral cowardice is the ruin of manhood – Numbers 13:33.

Double-mindedness: The double-minded waver between right and wrong because they are undecided – 1 Kings 18:21. They profess to hate sin but have a lingering love for it – James 4:1. They do not have a right understanding of good and evil – Hebrews 5:14.

Moral courage: Enables a person to encounter hatred, disapproval and contempt without departing from what is right – Psalm 119:157. Examples: John the Baptist – Matthew 14:3-10; Daniel – Daniel 6; David – 1 Samuel 17; Paul – Acts 27; 28:1-5; Stephen – Acts 7; Gideon – Judges 6, 7

3. Name some groups who are bold in their identification. *(page 37)*

a. _homosexuals_

b. _communism_

c. _Nazism_

4. When you lose your life, you'll find it. Look up and write out Matthew 16:25.

Self-help is no help at all. Self sacrifice is the way, my way, to finding yourself your true self

G. Life is composed of your ___choices___ and constructed by your ___words___. *(page 39)*

1. To hold the courage of your convictions, you need to _tell the difference b/t right + wrong_. *(page 39)*

2. Read: *"God is not ashamed to be called their God"* Hebrews 11:16.

What kind of man is that said about? *(page 39)* _____

_____

What kind of man do you want to be? _One that knows the Truth_

For Further Study

Boldness is a form of courage – Hebrews 13:6; Proverbs 10:10 TLB; 1 Peter 3:15. Successful men are bold in their identification with their belief, product or activity and in their confession of it – Psalm 119:46; Romans 1:16. Overcome fear of men, openly identify with Jesus and be bold in your confession of Him – *"And fear not them which kill the body, but are not able to kill the soul: but rather fear him which is able to destroy both soul and body in hell...Whosoever therefore shall confess me before men, him will I confess also before my Father which is in heaven"* Matthew 10:28, 32, 33; *"And they overcame him (the devil) by the blood of the Lamb, and by the word of their testimony; and they loved not their lives unto the death"* Revelation 12:11.
When we lose our life in identification with Jesus Christ, we find a greater life we would never have known otherwise – *"Whoever finds his [lower] life will lose it [the higher life], and whoever loses his [lower] life on My account will find it [the higher life]"* Matthew 10:39 AMP.

3. Read: *"I want you to be wise about what is right, and innocent about what is evil."* Romans 16:19 NIV.

4. *"Stop listening to teaching that contradicts what you know is* ___right___ *"* Proverbs 19:27 TLB. *(page 39)*

H. Men tend to judge others based on what they ___do___ and themselves by their _____. *(page 39)*

1. Intentions are not ___actions___. *(page 39)*

2. Every morning read a chapter of ___Proverbs___. *(page 40)*

3. Every evening read a chapter from ___Psalms___. *(page 40)*

For Further Study

Choices – *"Choose life!"* Deuteronomy 30:19; *"Death and life are in the power of the tongue"* Proverbs 18:21.
Don't be embarrassed about your commitment to God – Mark 8:38. Be bold in word and deed – Acts 4:13.
Learn to discern between good and evil, the truth and a lie – 1 Kings 3:9.
Don't be moved by every person's personality, persuasion and belief – Ephesians 4:14.
Don't listen to teaching which contradicts what you know is right – Proverbs 19:27.
Find a godly pastor who can help you and who can be your example in word, lifestyle, love, spirit, faith, purity
– Philippians 3:17, 18.
Judge yourself by your actions, not by your intentions – Proverbs 21:8.
Lay a right foundation for your character – 2 Corinthians 7:1.
The choice is yours; the glory is God's – 2 Peter 3:18.

Practical:

1. In what ways might I be church-wise or double-minded?

   _____

   _____

2. What do I need to start running away from?

   _____

   _____

Repeat this prayer out loud:

Father, in Jesus' Name, I will not be a double-minded man. I will be a man of decision and live a life pleasing unto You, full of moral courage. I will reverence the right and reject the wrong. I will hold fast to truth and let go of lies. Grant me boldness to proclaim my faith in my home, in my workplace, wherever I go. I will lose my life in identification with Christ that You might be glorified through me. Amen.

Principles I want to memorize:

Self Test *Lesson 4*

1. **In your own words,** write out a definition of moral cowardice.

   a. _____

   b. _____

2. Success is not based on the ability to say "_____" but on the ability to say "_____."

3. Write the names of three Bible men who showed moral courage.

   a. _____

   b. _____

   c. _____

4. You find your life by _____.

5. To be a real man, we must identify with _____.

Lesson 5
WIMPS: Made in America

Lesson 5
WIMPS: Made in America

A. Sanctify your ___ego___; don't kill it. *(page 41)*

B. Use the words below to complete the following phrases: *(pages 41-43)*

character	dreams	will	inferiority	weaknesses
humility	strengths	sin	personality	

1. You make a success out of your life by going to your ___strengths___, not concentrating on your ___weaknesses___.

2. "Religion" has said it is a ___sin___ to achieve great things.

3. The devil will usurp your ___character___ and ___humility___ and put you into ___inferiority___ if you allow him.

4. God fulfills His ___will___ by enabling you to realize your _____.

5. Many men heard _____ preached in church but saw _____ practiced.

For Further Study
Determine to follow after success and godliness – Deuteronomy 8:18.
Purify your motives and use your ego to achieve great things for God – Mark 12:30.
Concentrate on your strengths, not your weaknesses – Romans 12:6.
Beware of religion, the enemy of spiritual fulfillment – Matthew 15:6. Religion is the devil's counterfeit of Christianity, one of the tools Satan uses to destroy men and usurp their rightful position – John 10:10. Religion leads to the bondage of failure, poverty and mediocrity – Galatians 4:9.
Religion teaches that it is a sin to achieve great things; it preaches humility but practices inferiority – Colossians 2:8.
Religion causes men to bury their gifts, talents and abilities in an effort to achieve spirituality – Matthew 25:25.
Religion perpetuates error; men who build their lives on it will never fulfill the God-inspired goals for their lives – *"Except the Lord build the house, they labour in vain that build it"* Psalm 127:1.

C. God created men to be successful. *(page 43)* ___ True ___ False

D. Read the following and comment on how each can apply to your life:

1. *"Delight thyself also in the LORD; and he shall give thee the desires of thine heart"* Psalm 37:4. *(page 43)*

   _____

   _____

2. *"Kindness makes a man attractive"* Proverbs 19:22 TLB. *(page 47)*

   _____

3. *"The woman is the glory of the man"* 1 Corinthians 11:7b. *(page 47)*

   _____

4. *"Therefore to him that knoweth to do good, and doeth it not, to him it is sin"* James 4:17. *(page 49)*

   _____

   _____

For Further Study

Recognize that, as a man, you were created by God to be successful—a hero and a champion – Genesis 1:26.

Recognize your gifts, talents and abilities, and dedicate them to God – *"I beseech you therefore, brethren, by the mercies of God, that ye present your bodies a living sacrifice, holy, acceptable unto God, which is your reasonable service"* Romans 12:1.

Let God put creative ideas in your mind and godly desires in your heart – *"Delight thyself also in the Lord; and he shall give thee the desires of thine heart"* Psalm 37:4.

Let Him fulfill His will be enabling you to realize those dreams – *"Commit thy way unto the Lord; trust also in him; and he shall bring it to pass"* Psalm 37:5.

E. Women still want a real man, one who … *(circle the right phrase in each set) (page 47)*

1. rejects / accepts responsibility 3. is impulsive / is decisive

2. is egotistic / is chivalrous 4. shows courtesy and is kind / is abrupt

F. How can the woman be the glory of the man unless that man is _____

_____

_____? *(page 47)*

G. God calls each of us to live up to our own potential. *(pages 49)*

Look up, read and then comment on the following Scriptures:

1. Philippians 1:6 _____

_____

2. Ephesians 3:20 _____

_____

_____

For Further Study

Crucify the flesh, but live a resurrected life – *"For if we have been planted together in the likeness of his death, we shall be also in the likeness of his resurrection"* Romans 6:5.

Die to pride, fear and the vain things of the world and the flesh – *"Knowing this, that our old man is crucified with him, that the body of sin might be destroyed, that henceforth we should not serve sin"* Romans 6:6.

But live for God-given dreams, divinely-inspired desires which are realized through the resurrection power within you – *"Work out your own salvation with fear and trembling. For it is God which worketh in you both to will and to do of his good pleasure"* Philippians 2:12, 13.

Determine to live up to the potential that is within you, placed there by God – Philippians 3:12.

H. Getting rid of the wimp factor

1. Promotion doesn't come from the east or _____ but from _____. *(page 50)*
   Read: *"For promotion cometh neither from the east, nor from the west, nor from the south. But God is the judge: he putteth down one, and setteth up another"* Psalm 75:6, 7.

2. God didn't call us to be _____ but peacemakers. *(page 50)*

   Peace comes only through _____. *(page 50)*

3. Read: *"When the Lord your God delivers them over to you to be destroyed, do a complete job of it—don't make any treaties or show them mercy; utterly wipe them out"* Deuteronomy 7:2 TLB.

   What does that mean to you? _____

4. Men who _____, who settle for a _____ with their sins, live in misery.

   Only when they fight through to _____ do they live in peace. *(page 50)*

5. Satan wanted to compromise with Jesus, but Jesus fought through to total victory. The result is that He

   gives us _____. *(page 51)*

6. Read: *"And having spoiled principalities and powers, he made a show of them openly, triumphing over them in it"* Colossians 2:15.

I. Hearing from God depends on age. *(page 51)*   ___ True   ___ False

For Further Study

Depend upon God to promote you – Psalm 75:6, 7.
Trust that your gift will make a way for you – Proverbs 22:29.
Develop your own relationship with God – *"Even the Spirit of truth; whom the world cannot receive, because it seeth him not, neither knoweth him: but ye know him; for he dwelleth with you, and shall be in you"* John 14:17.
You are never too young to hear from God. Hearing from God doesn't depend on age but on relationship – *"My sheep hear my voice, and I know them, and they follow me"* John 10:27.
If you don't seek God's counsel, you may be deceived into making a truce with the enemy: Joshua and the Gibeonites – *"And the men took of their victuals, and asked not counsel at the mouth of the Lord. And Joshua made peace with them, and made a league with them, to let them live: and the princes of the congregation sware unto them"* Joshua 9:14, 15.

J. In the "substitute" society, men try to substitute... *(pages 53-54) (Write the letter in the blank that completes a correct sentence.)*

___	wishing	for	a.	primitive power of God's presence
___	truces	for	b.	faith
___	manners and culture	for	c.	reality
___	fantasy	for	d.	righteousness
___	respectability	for	e.	gentleness
___	works	for	f.	prayer
___	softness	for	g.	victory

For Further Study

Learn to identify wimps – *"Such persons claim they know God, but from seeing the way they act, one knows they don't"* Titus 1:16 TLB. They substitute manners and culture for the power of God's presence – 1 Corinthians 4:20. They substitute status symbols for the fruit of the Spirit – Colossians 3:2, 3; Matthew 13:22. They substitute fantasy for reality – Romans 1:25; Jeremiah 23; 24. They substitute respectability for righteousness – *"For they loved the praise of men more than the praise of God"* John 12:43; John 5:44. They substitute works for faith – *"But without faith it is impossible to please him"* Hebrews 11:6. They substitute softness for gentleness (God is tender, not soft) – Romans 2:4, 5.

Men who are soft – *"Ye have not yet resisted unto blood, striving against sin"* Hebrews 12:4. Soft men can't take rough times. They make truces and compromises with the flesh, the world and the devil – 1 Corinthians 10:13. Jesus was gentle but not soft. He taught a ruthlessness required by God – Mark 9:43, 44. Soft men don't have more because they settle for less (the children of Israel) – *"How long are ye slack to go to possess the land?"* Joshua 18:3. Soft men forfeit victory by seeking to avoid pain – 1 Corinthians 9:25.

K. The reason you don't have _____ is that you settle for _____. *(page 54)*

Practical:

1. Jesus said, "Whatever offends you, CUT IT OFF." What do you need to cut out of your life?

    _____

2. Joseph, David, Samson, Samuel, Daniel … How can you add your name to God's list of heroes?

    _____

    _____

Repeat this prayer out loud:

Father, in the Name of Jesus, open my eyes to see and truly understand the gifts and talents You have put in me. You want me to develop them, and I will start today. This day I decide to press into my Canaan Land and possess absolute victory in my life. I will not settle for a truce, or for second best, because You went all the way for me. I will do the same, that men might see Your grace at work in my life. Amen.

For Further Study

Don't be a wimp – *"Watch ye, stand fast in the faith, quit you like men, be strong"* 1 Corinthians 16:13. Don't compromise with sin. Fight until you have victory. Then you can live in peace – *"Wherefore take unto you the whole armour of God, that ye may be ale to withstand in the evil day, and having done all, to stand"* Ephesians 6:13.

Self Test *Lesson 5*

1. Your ego is an absolute enemy of your manhood; you must crucify it.   ___ True   ___ False

2. What is the difference between humility and inferiority?

    _____

    _____

    _____

3. The Bible teaches us to live a crucified life.   ___ True   ___ False

    If "True," explain:

    _____

    If "False," what kind of life are we to lead?

    _____

4. Absolute peace will come only through absolute _____.

5. Hearing from God doesn't depend upon _____ but upon relationship.

6. The reason you don't have _____ is because you settle for _____.

Lesson 6
Sex

Lesson 6
Sex

A. God made sex _____. *(page 57)*

A sinful man _____ sex. *(page 57)*

B. Among the purposes for sex are: *(circle one) (page 57)*

1. to replenish the earth

2. the power that holds the family together

3. to symbolize the spiritual union of marriage

4. for the mutual benefit and blessing of both a husband and wife

5. all of the above

C. List some reasons why God prohibits sex outside of marriage. *(page 57)*

1. _____

2. _____

3. _____

For Further Study
God made everything good, including sex – *"And God saw every thing that he had made, and, behold, it was very good"* Genesis 1:31.
God made sex as a means of replenishing the earth – *"And God blessed them, and God said unto them, Be fruitful, and multiply, and replenish the earth"* Genesis 1:28.
God made sexual energy the power that holds the family together – *"Therefore shall a man leave his father and his mother, and shall cleave unto his wife"* Genesis 2:24.
Sex is a physical union which symbolizes the spiritual union of man and woman – *"And they shall be one flesh"* Genesis 2:24.
God created sex so that a man and a woman in the union of marriage could give themselves unreservedly to each other – 1 Corinthians 7:4.

D. God's Word is full of warnings concerning unbridled passion. *(page 58)*

   1. Read Proverbs 2:16-19; 5:3-9; 7:4-27.

      Summarize these verses: _____

      _____

   2. List what God's Word does for our minds. *(page 58)*

      a. _____

      b. _____

   3. Read Romans 1. People changed the truth of God into a _____. *(page 58)*

   4. The first symptom of error is taking Scriptures and making them conform to your _____,

      instead of taking your _____ and making it conform to the Word of God. *(page 59)*

   5. Choose from these two words to complete the sentence: will   image
      (page 63)

      We submit to the _____ and _____ of God, not make God into our _____

      according to our _____.

For Further Study

God's prohibition on sex outside marriage was given to protect sex – *"Marriage is honourable in all, and the bed undefiled"* Hebrews 13:4.

The woman should be the glory of the man, not the object of his lust and thus the cause of his separation from God – 1 Corinthians 11:7.

God's Word is filled with warnings to young men concerning their unbridled passions – Proverbs 7:24, 25; *"Flee fornication…he that committeth fornication sinneth against his own body"* 1 Corinthians 6:18.

Programming the conscience: God's Word washes the mind and programs the conscience to righteousness – *"Christ also loved the church, and gave himself for it; That he might sanctify and cleanse it with the washing of water by the word"* Ephesians 5:25, 26; Psalm 119:9.

The first symptom of error – 2 Timothy 4:3, 4; Perversion of life leads to perversion of the Scriptures – Romans 1:24, 25. God never gave His Word so people could take it to justify their own lifestyles – Deuteronomy 12:32.

E. Draw a line between phrases to create the correct sentences. *(pages 63-64)*

1. God's Word is the source of your faith and   to the degree that obedience is exercised.

2. God's power is released   His love is unconditional.

3. God's promises are conditional and   the sole rule of conduct.

F. You cannot read pornographic materials or attend porn films without being affected by the unclean spirits that produced them.

1. All pornography is: *(circle one) (page 65)*

    a. natural   b. justifiable   c. permissible   d. idolatrous

2. Read: *"Don't you realize that you can choose your own master? You can choose sin (with death) or else obedience (with acquittal). The one to whom you offer yourself—he will take you and be your master and you will be his slave"* Romans 6:16 TLB.

    In what way does this relate to pornography? _____

    _____

For Further Study

God's Word is the source of faith – *"Man shall not live by bread alone, but by every word that proceedeth out of the mouth of God"* Matthew 4:4; Psalm 119:112.

God's power is released to the degree that obedience is exercised – Revelation 2:26.

God's promises are conditional – *"If ye be willing and obedient, ye shall eat the good of the land"* Isaiah 1:19.

The Holy Spirit is given to restrain the Christian so he is kept pure before God in thought, word and deed – *"And I will put my spirit within you, and cause you to walk in my statutes, and ye shall keep my judgments, and do them"* Ezekiel 36:27.

A person cannot engage in pornography without being affected by the unclean spirits which produced it – Proverbs 6:27, 28. Pornography becomes an idolatrous activity. The image is created in the mind of the viewer – Ezekiel 8:12. In turn, pornography creates a stronghold in the mind and a snare to the life – Psalm 106:36. Idolatrous fantasizing and private sex sins are a sin against one's own manhood – Deuteronomy 7:26.

G. Sin always promises to _____ and _____, but in reality, it always _____

and _____. *(page 67)*

"My guilt has overwhelmed me like a burden too heavy to bear. My wounds fester and are loathsome because of my sinful folly. I am bowed down and brought very low; all day long I go about mourning" Psalm 38:4-6 NIV.

"Your words are what sustain me; they are food to my hungry soul. They bring joy to my sorrowing heart and delight me. How proud I am to bear your name, O Lord" Jeremiah 15:16 TLB.

In what way do these two verses of Scripture compare/contrast? _____

_____

H. What does Jesus mean by saying, *"My yoke is easy, and My burden is light"* Matthew 11:30? *(page 68)*

_____

_____

_____

_____

For Further Study

Sin's deception: Sin promises to serve but creates bondage instead – *"Jesus answered them, Verily, verily, I say unto you, Whosoever committeth sin is the servant of sin"* John 8:34; 2 Peter 2:19.

Sin alters behavior – *"When the woman saw that the tree was good for food…she took of the fruit thereof, and did eat, and gave also to her husband…and he did eat. And the eyes of them both were opened, and they knew that they were naked; and they sewed fig leaves together, and made themselves aprons. And they heard the voice of the Lord God waling in the garden…and Adam and his wife hid themselves from the presence of the Lord God"* Genesis 3:6-8.

I. Finish Romans 8:1. *(page 68)*

"There is now no condemnation to them which are in Christ Jesus ...

_____."

Practical:

1. Two verses are quoted on pages 70-71. What do they mean to you?

    "He that is slow to anger is better than the mighty; and he that ruleth his spirit than he that taketh a city" Proverbs 16:32.

    _____

    _____

    _____

    "Thy word have I hid in mine heart, that I might not sin against thee" Psalm 119:11.

    _____

    _____

    _____

For Further Study

Submitting to God's yoke – Matthew 11:28, 29

Knowing that you have repented of known sin gives you an easy feeling – Romans 8:2.

You are light-hearted when you are not burdened with guilt – Psalm 32:5.

Being yoked to righteousness is a joy forever – *"Being then made free from sin, ye became the servants of righteousness"* Romans 6:18.

Freedom from sin allows God's glory and power to flow through your life – 1 John 3:21, 22.

To remain free from sin, program your conscience to righteousness by the Word of God – *"Let the word of Christ dwell in you richly in all wisdom"* Colossians 3:16.

Love God's Word – *"Oh how I love thy law! it is my meditation all the day"* Psalm 119:97.

Apply it to your life – *"If ye know these things, happy are ye if ye do them"* John 13:17.

2. Name three ways you can guard your heart from sexual temptation. *(page 71)*

_____

_____

_____

3. A man frequently goes to bars to drink with friends, then finds that he cannot control himself sexually with women he meets. Every Sunday, when he attends church, he asks God to forgive him, but almost every weekend, he fails. What steps could he take to change?

_____

_____

_____

Repeat this prayer out loud:

Father, in Jesus' Name, please help me keep myself sexually pure. I make a covenant with my eyes not to look at pornographic imagery of any kind. I choose to walk free from the addictions and bondage of lust and to keep myself available to You. I thank You that You will not allow me to be tempted beyond my ability to resist. I am strong in Your grace, and I will keep myself for Your work. Amen.

Principles I want to memorize:

Self Test   *Lesson 6*

1. God's power is released to the degree that _____ is exercised and no more.

2. God is adamant about no sex outside of marriage. What are some of the problems caused by disobedience in this area?

    a. _____

    b. _____

    c. _____

    d. _____

3. Reading God's Word regularly will eventually _____ _____.

4. We are to take Scriptures and make them conform to our lifestyle.   ___ True   ___ False

5. All _____ is idolatrous.

6. All sin promises to _____ and to _____, but in reality, it always _____

    and _____.

Lesson 7
How Do You Spell "Release"?

Lesson 7
How Do You Spell "Release"?

A. Look up John 20:22-23 and write out the verses. _____

_____

_____

_____

1. "Retain" means to "hold fast to" or "keep possession of." What is retained through unforgiveness?

    (page 76) _____

2. Simple truth *(page 76)*: If you forgive, you _____. If you do not _____, you retain.

B. Read: *"And be ye kind one to another, tenderhearted, forgiving one another, even as God for Christ's sake hath forgiven you"* Ephesians 4:32.

1. Is forgiveness an option or a command? _____

2. Is forgiveness based on obedience or feelings? _____

For Further Study

The principal of release (John 20:22, 23) states that only after sins are released are people free to become what God wants them to be – Matthew 6:14, 15. Remember: The sins you forgive are released, and the sins you do not forgive are retained in your life – *"[Now, having received the Holy Spirit and being led and directed by Him] if you forgive the sins of anyone they are forgiven; if you retain the sins of anyone, they are retained"* John 20:23 AMP.

Healing takes place when, by faith, the principle of release is acted upon – *"Let us lay aside every weight, and the sin which doth so easily beset us, and let us run with patience the race that is set before us"* Hebrews 12:1.

In order to activate this principle in your life, admit the Holy Spirit into your heart, and be guided and directed by Him – *"Then Jesus...breathed on them and said to them, Receive (admit) the Holy Spirit!"* John 20:21, 22 AMP.

C. Who is responsible for your life? *(page 81)* _____

    1. What important relationship helped shape your life? *(pages 80-83)*

       _____

    2. What does God require of you in that relationship? *(pages 84-85)*

       _____

    3. Read: *"And whenever you stand praying, if you have anything against anyone, forgive him and let it drop (leave it, let it go), in order that your Father Who is in heaven may also forgive you your [own] failings and shortcomings and let them drop"* Mark 11:25 AMP.

D. If "Christianity is not religion," what is it? *(circle one) (page 84)*

    a relationship   a series of oaths to live by   a dogma

    Briefly explain. _____

    _____

For Further Study

The doorway to maturity:

Maturity doesn't come with age; it comes with acceptance of responsibility – *"And when he had removed him, he raised up unto them David to be their king; to whom also he gave testimony, and said, I have found David the son of Jesse, a man after mine own heart, which shall fulfil all my will"* Acts 13:22.

We cannot mature if we go through life blaming circumstances, or other people, for our shortcomings – Proverbs 16:2; 21:2; Genesis 3:11, 12.

We alone are responsible for our own life – *"For we must all appear before the judgment seat of Christ; that every one may receive the things done in his body, according to that he hath done, whether it be good or bad"* 2 Corinthians 5:10.

E. Men are required to _____ their fathers. *(page 84)*

1. To rebel against fathers is to invite _____. *(page 84)*

2. To rebel against a sinful father allows his sins to _____ your life. *(pages 84-85)*

F. You do only two things in life: _____ and _____. *(page 85)*

1. How you _____ determines how you _____. *(page 85)*

2. What should you never take to the next stage, relationship or situation of your life? *(page 86)*

_____

_____

G. Each leaving and entering process creates _____ in our lives. Therefore _____ is normal to life. *(page 86)*

1. Read: *"Dear friends, don't be bewildered or surprised when you go through the fiery trials ahead, for this is no strange, unusual thing that is going to happen to you"* 1 Peter 4:12 TLB.

For Further Study

The importance of the father/son relationship:
The Word of God talks about fathers and sons in various ways – Proverbs 17:6; 20:7; *"Reverence for God gives a man deep strength; his children have a place of refuge and security"* Proverbs 14:26 TLB. Fathers have a God-given responsibility to their offspring. Fathers are blessed when they raise their children in the fear and admonition of the Lord – Deuteronomy 11:18-21. Fathers are cursed if they neglect their family responsibility – Proverbs 17:25. Sons also have responsibilities toward their fathers. They are to honor their fathers – Ephesians 6:2; Proverbs 20:20. They are to submit to their father's authority in the Lord – Colossians 3:20. They are not to allow their father's sins to ruin their life – Hebrews 12:15. They are to make sure their heart is clean before God concerning their father, forgiving him of his sins, offenses and neglect – Ephesians 4:31, 32.

2. All crisis has an element of _____ in it. *(page 86)*

   All true joy is born out of _____. *(page 86)*

   a. The _____ of graduation comes from the _____ of study and homework. *(page 86)*

   b. The _____ of salvation is known after the experience of _____

   _____ for your sins which leads to repentance. *(page 86)*

3. Don't let crises separate you from _____. *(page 86)*

   Let God take you through the crisis to the next _____. *(page 88)*

Practical:

1. Read: *"Therefore, if you are offering your gift at the altar and there remember that your brother has something against you, leave your gift there in front of the altar. First go and be reconciled to your brother; then come and offer your gift"* Matthew 5:23-24 NIV.

   What does this verse mean to you? _____

   _____

For Further Study

How you leave determines how you enter – *"Be not deceived; God is not mocked: for whatsoever a man soweth, that shall he also reap"* Galatians 6:7.

How you leave one sphere or experience of life will determine how you enter the next – *"For so an entrance shall be ministered unto you abundantly into the everlasting kingdom of our Lord and Saviour Jesus Christ. Wherefore I will not be negligent to put you always in remembrance of these things, though ye know them, and be established in the present truth"* 2 Peter 1:10, 11.

2. To rid yourself of sins—both your own sins and those committed against you—you must forgive.

    a. Name people to forgive whose sins you immediately think of.

    _____

    b. Make an appointment between yourself and God to forgive them.

    c. Name secondary people you didn't think of and do the same. Here are some ideas:

scout leader	teacher	coach	childhood friend
neighbor	school bully	church leader	television teacher

3. If you are a father, go to your children, and ask them to forgive you of your mistakes and sins against them. Help their future be unhindered by your past.
    If you are a son whose father is alive, go to him and ask him to forgive you of your mistakes and sins against him. Help your future be unhindered by that past relationship.

    NOTE: *If the person you need to forgive has passed away, you can write out a letter to rid yourself of past sins. Also of note, it is not unusual, as you practice forgiveness, to find that you are angry with God. Even though He does not require forgiveness because He is perfect, YOU may require the act of forgiving Him to make your relationship with Him right again.*

For Further Study
Change produces crisis in life.
Crisis is normal to life – *"In the world ye shall have tribulation"* John 16:33.
Crisis has sorrow in it, but sorrow is life's greatest teacher – Ecclesiastes 7:3; *"It is good for me that I have been afflicted; that I might learn thy statutes"* Psalm 119:71.
All true joy is born out of sorrow – *"They that sow in tears shall reap in joy"* Psalm 126:5; *"Weeping may endure for a night, but joy cometh in the morning"* Psalm 30:5.
God wants every change in the lives of His children to be good – Romans 8:28.

Repeat this prayer out loud:

Father, by faith and in accordance with Your Word, I receive Your Holy Spirit power into my life. By the ability of Your Spirit, and by the authority of Your Word, I forgive myself for every sin I've ever committed, and I forgive _____ for their sins against me. I release them out of my life. I don't want to bear those sins any longer, so I forgive everybody. Make me free, Lord, to be the man You want me to be. Thank You, Lord. In Jesus' Name, Amen.

For Further Study

Learn to take advantage of the crises in your life.

Don't let crises separate you from God. Use them to bring you closer to Him. Let God take you through each crisis to the next stage of life – *"For I am persuaded, that neither death, nor life, nor angels, nor principalities, nor powers, nor things present, nor things to come, Nor height, nor depth, nor any other creature, shall be able to separate us from the love of God, which is in Christ Jesus our Lord"* Romans 8:38, 39.

Always remember that God is for you, not against you – *"When I cry unto thee, then shall mine enemies turn back: this I know; for God is for me"* Psalm 56:9.

Be careful not to waste your youth brooding over what someone else has done to you – *"Remember ye not the former things, neither consider the things of old"* Isaiah 43:18.

Self Test *Lesson 7*

1. **In your own words**, write a definition of the "Principle of Release."

   _____

   _____

   _____

2. Where is the principle found in Scripture? _____

3. Who is ultimately responsible for your life? *(circle one)*

   a.   my pastor

   b.   God

   c.   myself

4. To honor your father and mother is the first commandment with _____.

5. There are really only two things that you do in life: _____ and _____.

6. Crisis is normal to life.   ___ True   ___ False

7. All true joy is born out of _____.

8. To not forgive someone of their sin against you, no matter how painful, is to _____ the sin to yourself.

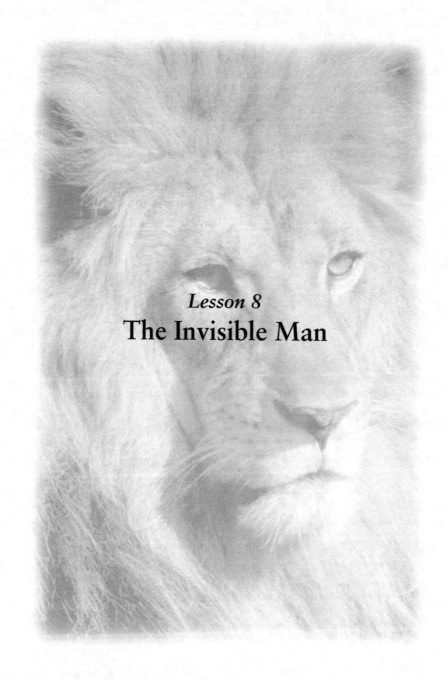

Lesson 8
The Invisible Man

Lesson 8
The Invisible Man

A. Define "courage." *(page 91)* _____

_____

   1. Every decision a man makes is based on _____. *(page 91)*

   2. The decisions of your life either _____ or _____ your
      character. *(page 91)*

B. What is the difference between personality and character? *(page 91)* _____

_____

When _____ wears off, only _____ remains. *(page 92)*

For Further Study

Character is built in private. It develops out of a lifetime of individual decisions which either enhance or diminish it –"*I have chosen the way of truth: thy judgments have I laid before me*" Psalm 119:30; "*If a man therefore purge himself from these, he shall be a vessel unto honour, sanctified, and meet for the master's use, and prepared unto every good work*" 2 Timothy 2:21.

Character and personality: Personality is not the same as character – Proverbs 26:23. Personality is after the outward man and is temporal – 1 Samuel 16:7.

Character and the honor of God: Obedience to His Word honors God; disobedience dishonors Him – Proverbs 14:2; 1 Samuel 15:22, 23.

Faith in God honors Him; unbelief dishonors Him –"*But without faith it is impossible to please him: for he that cometh to God must believe that he is, and that he is a rewarder of them that diligently seek him*" Hebrews 11:6.

C. When you _____ God _____, you'll make good decisions _____. *(page 92)*

1. Name three ways you honor God. *(page 92)*

   a. _____

   b. _____

   c. _____

2. Read: *"But now the Lord says: 'Far be it from Me; for those who honor Me I will honor, and those who despise Me shall be lightly esteemed'"* 1 Samuel 2:30 NKJV.

   God _____ those who _____ Him. *(page 92)*

D. Name something that courageous men believe is more important than life itself. *(page 94)*

   _____

1. Read Daniel 3.

2. Read Genesis 39 and 41.
   At first, Joseph ended up in prison. How long did he stay? _____

For Further Study

Trust in Jesus as Savior honors God; rejection of the Son dishonors the Father – John 6:29; *"And he that despiseth me (Jesus) despiseth him that sent me"* Luke 10:16.

God is honored when His children refuse to succumb to temptation – James 1:12.

A man who has learned to honor God privately will show good character in his decisions publicly – *"I have refrained my feet from every evil way, that I might keep thy word. I have not departed from thy judgments: for thou hast taught me…Through thy precepts I get understanding: therefore I hate every false way"* Psalm 119:101, 102, 104.

Examples of men who honored God: Mordecai – He was elevated by God to the office of prime minister (Esther 2:21, 22; 10:3); Shadrach, Meshach and Abednego – They were promoted and prospered (Daniel 3:16-18, 30); Joseph – He became second in command to Pharaoh (Genesis 39:7-12; 41:39, 40).

God honors those who honor Him – 1 Samuel 2:30 TLB; Psalm 91:14, 15; John 12:26.

How did God honor Joseph? *(circle one)* *(page 95)*
a. gave him a desirable wife
b. by promoting him to the highest government position in a country where he was an alien
c. both of the above

In your opinion, was it worth the time in prison?   ___ Yes   ___ No

3. Sin is always a form of insanity. *(page 96)*   ___ True   ___ False

4. Look up and read Luke 4:14. When Jesus overcame temptation, He returned:

"_____." *(page 96)*

5. Name some of the benefits of honoring God. *(page 96)* _____

_____

6. Read: *"Why do you honor your sons more than me by fattening yourselves on the choice parts of every offering made by my people Israel?"* 1 Samuel 2:29b NIV.

Who is this story about? _____

For Further Study
When a man honors God, he strengthens his character, increases the stature of his manhood and finds favor with God and man – Job 17:9; Psalms 84:5, 7; 89:17; Proverbs 4:18; Luke 2:40, 52.
The honor of God is the criterion for the Christian way of living – Ecclesiastes 12:13.
All sin is deceitful – *"But exhort one another daily, while it is called Today; lest any of you be hardened through the deceitfulness of sin"* Hebrews 3:13.
The Christian must know the truth so he can recognize the lies of Satan and fight for the honor of God – Proverbs 2:6-9. God's Word is the source of truth – John 17:7. God's Spirit guides into all truth – *"Howbeit when he, the Spirit of truth, is come, he will guide you into all truth"* John 16:13.
Honesty is the core of integrity – Proverbs 11:3, 5.
The upright are directed by their honesty; the wicked shall fall beneath their load of sin – Proverbs 12:5, 13.
God loves honesty but hates cheating – Proverbs 11:1.

E. God's Word tells us that Satan is the _____. *(page 100)*

1. Because of that, all sin is _____ in its character. *(page 101)*

2. You must have _____ so that you can recognize _____. *(page 101)*

F. Use the following words to fill in the blanks below:

temptation   pray   prayer   boldness

commission   courage   private   omission

1. The sin of _____ is as great as the sin of _____. *(page 103)*

2. Neglecting to _____ will separate you from God as much as giving in to

_____. *(page 103)*

3. The result of _____ in _____ will be a life of _____

and _____ in public. *(page 103)*

For Further Study

God deals with His children according to His Word, not according to society's norm – *"There is a way that seemeth right unto a man, but the end thereof are the ways of death"* Proverbs 16:25.

The man who wants to follow God's Word and live his life in purity will find acceptance with God but not always with his peers – Psalm 119:51, 61, 63, 65.

As Christians, the honor of God should be more important to us than the honor of our peers – John 5:44.

If you are a child of God, don't submit your personal character to the character of your peer group – Exodus 23:2, 3.

If you make a quality decision to honor God in your thoughts, words, motives and deeds, God will honor you – *"If any man serve me, let him follow me; and where I am, there shall also my servant be: if any man serve me, him will my Father honour"* John 12:26.

G. You cannot gain by sacrifice what you lose through disobedience. *(page 104)*   ___ True   ___ False

H. Complete the sentence: God hates those who say that _____

    _____. *(page 106)*

Practical:

1. *"Can a man take fire in his bosom, and his clothes not be burned?"* Proverbs 6:27. *(page 99)*

    In your own words, explain how that verse of Scripture relates to your friendships.

    _____

    _____

    What will you do as a result? _____

For Further Study

Prayer: Prayer requires honesty with God – Psalm 51:6; *"The Lord is nigh unto all them that call upon him…in truth"* Psalm 145:18. True prayer is sharing with God the cares and needs of our lives and letting Him share with us His concern for the world – Philippians 4:6; *"Call unto me, and I will answer thee, and show thee great and mighty things, which thou knowest not"* Jeremiah 33:3. It is normal to pray – Luke 18:1; Ephesians 6:18. Neglect of prayer will separate us from God as much as yielding to temptation – 2 Chronicles 15:2.
Prayer leads to friendship with God. Friendship with God is life's greatest treasure – Psalm 25:14; Proverbs 3:32. Being with God dispels loneliness – *"I desire no one on earth as much as you!"* Psalm 73:25, 26 TLB.
Prayer leads to power with God. Men who know how to pray develop a boldness toward life that enables them to be more than conquerors – James 5:16, 17; *"If God be for us, who can be against us?…we are more than conquerors"* Romans 8:31, 37. Those who know how to pray know that God is for them – Psalm 56:9. The result of prayer in private is a life of boldness and courage in public – *"And when they had prayed,…they spake the word of God with boldness"* Acts 4:31.

2. Look up and write out the definition of "integrity." _____

   _____

3. What is prayer? *(page 101)* _____

   _____

4. The title of this chapter is "The Invisible Man." What is invisible? What is visible? How does it relate to giving? How does it relate to you? *(pages 103-104)*

   _____

   _____

   _____

Repeat this prayer out loud:

Father, I want to be a man who honors You and one whom You can honor. I recognize the insanity of sinning against You and understand the bitter results. I choose to honor You, that all may know that I am Yours. I choose to work on my character in my private life, that in my public life Your grace in me might be seen. Help me to read Your Word and pray daily. Help me to form good habits that honor You even in private. Thank You for strengthening me right now, in Jesus' Name, Amen.

For Further Study

The visible and the invisible – Prayer is an invisible tool which is wielded in a visible world: The Apostle Peter – Acts 12:4, 5, 7. The natural world is made up of the elements of the supernatural world. That which is visible is made up of that which is invisible – Hebrews 11:3.

Love is invisible; giving is visible – *"For God so loved the world, that he gave his only begotten Son, that whosoever believeth in him should not perish, but have everlasting life"* John 3:16.

Honor is invisible; obedience is visible – Luke 6:46. The degree of invisible love is evidenced by the degree of visible giving – *"Hereby perceive we the love of God, because he laid down his life for us: and we ought to lay down our lives for the brethren"* 1 John 3:16.

The quality of love for God is also reflected in obedience – John 14:21.

Giving cannot be a substitute for obedience – 1 Samuel 15:22; Proverbs 21:27. Honoring God results in both giving and obedience.

Self Test   *Lesson 8*

1. The most important part of my life is my personality.   ___ True   ___ False

2. When the personality is gone, only the _____ of a man remains.

3. What can a man do privately that results in God honoring him publicly?

   a. _____   b. _____

4. List some Biblical men who placed the honor of God above the value of their lives:

   a. _____ and _____

   b. _____

   c. _____

   d. _____

5. Name at least one man from the Bible who did not honor God. _____

   What were the results?

   ___ Good   ___ Bad   ___ Didn't make any difference

6. A major reason a man will have a life of boldness and courage in public life is that he will have "what" in his private life?

   _____

7. You can gain from sacrifice what you may have lost through disobedience.   ___ True   ___ False

Lesson 9
Working Hard, Going Nowhere

Lesson 9
Working Hard, Going Nowhere

A. Men often want _____ without _____. *(page 107)*

1. What are the six things a man is accountable for in life? *(page 108)*

   a. _____   c. _____   e. _____

   b. _____   d. _____   f. _____

2. Where will the truth be found that will lead you to be accountable for each of these six areas? *(circle one) (page 108)*

   a. sermons   b. friends   c. Bible   d. small groups

3. Truth is the bedrock of your _____. Your personal _____ is the cornerstone of your character. *(page 108)*

   Define "integrity" **in your own words.**

   _____

   _____

For Further Study

Every man has to face accountability for his own actions – *"So then every one of us shall give account of himself to God"* Romans 14:12; Luke 12:48.

Desire for authority without the willingness to accept accountability for one's actions leads to a no-growth situation – Proverbs 28:13.

Every man is accountable for six areas of responsibility in his own life (1 Timothy 3:1-11): Reputation – *"Abstain from all appearance of evil"* 1 Thessalonians 5:22; 2 Corinthians 6:3; Ethics – 1 Timothy 4:16; Morality – 2 Timothy 2:22; Temperament – 2 Timothy 2:24, 25; Habits – 1 Timothy 4:8; Maturity – 1 Timothy 4:15.

Truth is not an option in life – Zechariah 8:16. Truth is the bedrock of integrity. Your personal integrity is the cornerstone of your character – Psalm 24:4, 5. You receive God's own goodness as your blessing from Him, planted in your life by God Himself, your Savior.

4. *"Behold, thou desirest truth in the inward parts: and in the hidden part thou shalt make me to know wisdom"* Psalm 51:6.

   "The LORD shall judge the peoples; Judge me, O LORD, according to my righteousness, And according to my integrity within me" Psalm 7:8 NKJV.

   "The integrity of the upright guides them, but the unfaithful are destroyed by their duplicity" Proverbs 11:3 NIV.

   What do these verses have in common? _____

   What is God telling men in such verses? _____

5. The more you base your life on _____, the better will be your way and the greater will be

   your _____. The more you base your life on _____, the _____ will be

   your way and the _____ will be your life. *(page 108)*

6. Name some of the benefits and positive aspects of truth. *(page 109)*

   a. _____   d. _____

   b. _____   e. _____

   c. _____

For Further Study

The more you base your life on truth, the better will be your way and the greater will be your life – *"He that walketh uprightly walketh surely"* Proverbs 10:9; *"Jesus saith unto him, I am the way, the truth, and the life: no man cometh unto the Father, but by me"* John 14:6.

The more you base your life on a lie, the harder will be your way, and the less significant will be your life – *"The way of transgressors is hard"* Proverbs 13:15; Proverbs 2:22.

Truth is impartial – *"But the wisdom that is from above is...without partiality"* James 3:17.

Truth is eternal—it will stand firm – Proverbs 12:19.

Truth eliminates guilt, fear and secrecy. Truth brings freedom – *"And ye shall know the truth, and the truth shall make you free"* John 8:32.

Men may know the truth, recognize the truth and even admit to the truth yet still fall for deception if they do not love the truth – 2 Thessalonians 2:10; Titus 2:7.

7. Read: *"And with all deceivableness of unrighteousness in them that perish; because they received not the love of the truth, that they might be saved. And for this cause God shall send them strong delusion, that they should believe a lie: That they all might be damned who believed not the truth, but had pleasure in unrighteousness"* 2 Thessalonians 2:10-12.

How does that verse apply to your life? _____

_____

B. Look up and write out 2 Timothy 2:2.

_____

_____

_____

1. What major mistake do we often make in looking for men to serve God? *(page 109)*

_____

For Further Study

If a person loves the truth, he will make it a part of his life – *"Receive with meekness the engrafted word, which is able to save your souls. But be ye doers of the word, and not hearers only, deceiving your own selves"* James 1:21, 22; Titus 2:7.

Faithfulness – *"Moreover it is required in stewards, that a man be found faithful"* 1 Corinthians 4:2.

Faithfulness is the cornerstone of success – *"A faithful man shall abound with blessings"* Proverbs 28:20; Matthew 24:46, 47.

God commits to character, not to talent – *"Well done, thou good and faithful servant: thou hast been faithful over a few things, I will make thee ruler over many things: enter thou into the joy of thy Lord"* Matthew 25:21; Luke 16:10; 2 Timothy 2:2.

2. Read: *"I gave my brother Hanani, and Hananiah the ruler of the palace, charge over Jerusalem: for he was a faithful man, and feared God above many"* Nehemiah 7:2.

   What is this an example of? *(page 109)* _____

3. God commits to _____, not _____. *(page 109)*

4. God is looking for three other virtues in your manhood. *(page 111)*

   a. _____   b. _____   c. moral _____

C. What makes a nation great is not the virtue of her _____, but the wealth of her

   _____. *(page 113)*

D. The hardest thing for a man to do is _____. *(page 113)*

E. Read 1 Timothy 5:22.

   You must not allow yourself to _____ of another man's sins. *(page 113)*

For Further Study

Inconsistency is a mark of immaturity – *"That we henceforth be no more children, tossed to and fro, and carried about with every wind of doctrine"* Ephesians 4:14. Inconsistency takes a heavy toll on you and on those who depend on you – Proverbs 25:19. Don't waste your youth by inconsistent thinking and behavior – Ecclesiastes 12:1. Instead, be committed to spiritual growth. Take the time necessary to develop holiness, wisdom and proficiency – 1 Timothy 4:7, 8.

The mature person is willing to admit he is wrong and to change – Proverbs 28:13. Spiritual maturity requires a willingness to leave behind old friendships and associations that would bind us to the world or our past life – *"Do not be misled: 'Bad company corrupts good character'"* 1 Corinthians 15:33 NIV; 2 Corinthians 6:14.

To be true to God and yourself, you must find and fulfill His unique plan and purpose for your life – *"For we are his workmanship, created in Christ Jesus unto good works, which God hath before ordained that we should walk in them"* Ephesians 2:10.

1. What are the four most powerful motivations in the world? *(page 115)*

   a. _____   c. _____

   b. _____   d. _____

   Circle the one that is most powerful of all.

2. The qualities of love are the same as the virtues of manhood. What are they? *(page 115)*

   a. _____   d. _____   g. _____

   b. _____   e. _____   h. _____

   c. _____   f. _____   i. _____

3. Love centers in the feelings. *(page 116)*   ___ True   ___ False

---

For Further Study

You must not allow others to force you into their patterns of living. Learn from other people, but seek God to find the individual pattern He has for you alone – *"Don't let the world around you squeeze you into its own mould, but let God re-make you"* Romans 12:2 Phillips.

Do not allow yourself to partake of other men's sins, but follow after the Spirit of God – *"Lay hands suddenly on no man, neither be partaker of other men's sins: keep thyself pure"* 1 Timothy 5:22; *"But thou, O man of God, flee these things; and follow after righteousness"* 1 Timothy 6:11.

Love is the only motivation that is greater than the motivations of the world—fear, hate and greed – *"There is no fear in love; but perfect love casteth out fear"* 1 John 4:18; *"Love covers over a multitude of sins"* 1 Peter 4:8 NIV. Most of what is called love today is really lust – 1 John 2:15, 16.

Practical:

1. Read: *"Most men will proclaim every one his own goodness: but a faithful man who can find?"* Proverbs 20:6.
   "A faithful man shall abound with blessings: but he that maketh haste to be rich shall not be innocent" Proverbs 28:20.

   What can you do within the next month to draw your life in line with these verses?

   _____

   _____

2. What is the most powerful motivation for doing right for God?

   _____

Repeat this prayer out loud:

Father, I desire to be a faithful man. I admit where I've been wrong, stubborn and rebellious and ask for Your forgiveness. Help me choose friends and make decisions that will lead me into a more honorable walk with You. I want to be a mighty man of God, and I commit myself to that goal again today. Amen.

For Further Study

The qualities of love – Patience: *"Love is very patient"*; Kindness: *"and kind"*; Humility: *"never boastful or proud"*; Generosity: *"never selfish"*; Courtesy: *"or rude"*; Unselfishness: *"does not demand its own way"*; Temperance: *"is not irritable"*; Guilelessness: *"rejoices whenever truth wins out"*; Sincerity: *"will always believe in (the other person),…always expect the best of him"* 1 Corinthians 13:4-7 TLB.

These qualities are the virtues of the real man – *"But speaking the truth in love, (we) may grow up into him in all things, which is the head, even Christ"* Ephesians 4:15. The love of God put in your heart by the Holy Ghost can produce these elements in your life – Romans 5:5.

God can command His children to love because love centers in the will, not the emotions – *"I demand that you love each other as much as I love you"* John 15:12 TLB. To be a man after God's own heart, turn your heart toward love. Rid yourself of every other motivation – 1 Timothy 1:5. Allow the love of God to motivate you in your manhood as it motivated Jesus when He walked the earth as the Son of man – 2 Corinthians 5:14, 15.

Self Test *Lesson 9*

1. Many men want authority without _____.

2. Paul gave Timothy six things he was responsible for. List all six.

   a. _____   d. _____

   b. _____   e. _____

   c. _____   f. _____

3. Your personal _____ is the cornerstone of your character.

4. The more you base your life on _____, the _____ will be your way, and the greater will be your life.

5. What does God commit to? *(circle one)*

   a. talent   b. character   c. personality

6. Name the four most powerful motivations in the world.

   a. _____   c. _____

   b. _____   d. _____

7. Which of these four motivations, in our book, called "the toughest substance known to man," conquers the other three?

   _____

Lesson 10
Bend, Bow or Burn

Lesson 10
Bend, Bow or Burn

A. _____ and being alone are two entirely different things. *(page 118)*

_____ is sometimes necessary, even healthy and desirable.

1. Read: *"And when he had sent the multitudes away, he went up into a mountain apart to pray: and when the evening was come, he was there alone"* Matthew 14:23.

   This is a good example of a time someone would need to _____.

2. Write the correct letter in the blank that completes the sentence. *(page 117-118)*

   ___ suicide is   a. necessary and healthy

   ___ loneliness is   b. the antidote to loneliness

   ___ friends are   c. one of man's basic desires

   ___ being alone is   d. an epidemic in the United States

   ___ to belong is   e. never desirable

For Further Study

Loneliness and being alone: The Lord Jesus Christ – Matthew 14:23

Loneliness is never desirable – *"I looked on my right hand, and beheld, but there was no man that would know me: refuge failed me; no man cared for my soul"* Psalm 142:4.

The antidote to loneliness – *"Ointment and perfume rejoice the heart: so doth the sweetness of a man's friend by hearty counsel"* Proverbs 27:9.

Friends are Heaven's riches – Proverbs 17:17.

The desire to belong represents one of the most basic needs of man – Genesis 2:18.

Rejection is one of life's cruelest blows: The Lord Jesus Christ – *"He came unto his own, and his own received him not"* John 1:11; Isaiah 53:3.

A feeling of rejection is often the root cause of suicide: Elijah – 1 Kings 19:4, 10.

Finding healing in the ministry of Jesus – Psalm 34:18; The ministry of the Lord Jesus to the human heart completely heals the trauma of loneliness, failure and rejection – Luke 4:18.

B.   Overcoming _____ is one of life's greatest feats. *(page 118)*

   1.   The ministry of the Lord Jesus Christ to the human heart is to heal completely the trauma of: *(page 120)*

      a. _____   b. _____   c. _____

   2.   Look up: *"The Spirit of the Lord is upon me, because he hath anointed me to preach the gospel to the poor;*

      _____,

      to preach deliverance to the captives, and recovering of sight to the blind, to set at liberty them that are bruised" Luke 4:18.

C.   Read Daniel 3.
     The three Hebrews chose to _____ rather than be intimidated into _____. *(page 121)*

   1.   Read: *"Don't you realize that you can choose your own master? You can choose sin (with death) or else obedience (with acquittal). The one to whom you offer yourself—he will take you and be your master and you will be his slave"* Romans 6:16 TLB.

      What does that verse of Scripture mean in light of peer pressure or temptations you may feel?

      _____

For Further Study

The Lord's healing, acceptance, power and grace give the believer the ability to face the world and its reality – *"Yea, though I walk through the valley of the shadow of death, I will fear no evil: for thou art with me; thy rod and thy staff they comfort me. Thou preparest a table before me in the presence of mine enemies: thou anointest my head with oil; my cup runneth over"* Psalm 23:4, 5. Jesus gives a peace, an inner stability, that is a mystery to the world but a comfort to the believer – *"Peace I leave with you, my peace I give unto you: not as the world giveth, give I unto you. Let not your heart be troubled, neither let it be afraid"* John 14:27; Philippians 4:7.
In order to know the peace that passes all understanding, every area of life must be completely yielded to the Spirit of God – Romans 8:6. Holding on to any sin will create confusion that will prevent experiencing God's peace – 1 Peter 3:11, 12.
Because of man's intense desire to be accepted and belong, there is always pressure upon him to go along with the gang – Proverbs 1:10, 15.

2. The power of things you yield to in life grows _____, while what you resist

grows _____. *(page 121)*

3. Success in life is based on saying "yes"! *(page 121)*   ___ True   ___ False

4. The freedom to _____ between _____ is the _____ true freedom
you have. *(page 124)*

5. Your choices are shown in the _____ you keep. *(page 125)*

D. The following phrases describe: *(check which applies) (page 126)*

_____ church-wise   **or**   _____ street-wise

hard of heart   deceptive in spirit   con parents   do things to impress

manipulative   insolent in manner   religious

E. Purity is always popular in: *(circle one) (page 127)*

public schools   youth groups   adult classes   Heaven

1. The closest thing we can get to Heaven is to "keep thyself _____." *(page 127)*

For Further Study

What you submit to grows stronger – *"Submit yourselves therefore to God. Resist the devil, and he will flee from you"* James 4:7. Being intimidated into doing wrong weakens the resolve to do right – Romans 6:16. The more an individual says "yes" to the things that are right, the greater his ability to say "no" to wrong – Galatians 5:16. This power to resist wrong is the key to success. Jesus Christ overcame temptation with the Word of God – Luke 4:4, 8, 12. His submission to the Father, resistance to the devil and refusal to sin strengthened His spirit – Luke 4:14. To succeed in life as Jesus did, we must influence people to conform to our godly standard of behavior – Romans 12:2.

Choices – *"I call heaven and earth to record this day against you, that I have set before you life and death, blessing and cursing: therefore choose life, that both thou and thy seed may live"* Deuteronomy 30:19.

The freedom to choose between alternatives is the only true freedom in life – Galatians 5:13.

As Christians, we can choose to succeed or to fail; we can be wise or ignorant – Psalm 90:12.

Our choices are shown by the company we keep – Proverbs 27:19.

2. Fill in: *(pages 128-129)*

   a. Like begets _____.

   b. The common bond of rebels is their _____.

   c. Sin is _____; righteousness is _____.

   d. Make Jesus your _____.

   e. _____ is normal to life.

3. What makes a marriage work between times of passion? *(page 131)* _____

4. The common bond of friends is their _____. *(page 131)*

5. The greatness of God and Moses' friendship was not that Moses trusted God but that _____

   _____. *(page 131)*

F. What right comes from the right of possession? *(page 131)* _____

   1. What does God expect from men? *(page 132)* _____

   2. On what is our relationship with God based? *(page 133)* _____

For Further Study

Avoid the "church-wise" – Proverbs 13:20; Psalm 50:16, 17; *"Wherefore the Lord said,…this people draw near me with their mouth, and with their lips do honour me, but have removed their heart far from me, and their fear toward me is taught by the precept of men"* Isaiah 29:13.

Heaven is not reserved for the church-wise; it is the reward of the righteous. Only obedient spirits are allowed into Heaven – *"Who shall ascend into the hill of the Lord? or who shall stand in his holy place? He that hath clean hands, and a pure heart"* Psalm 24:3, 4. Purity is the rule of the day in Heaven – Job 31:1. God looks not at the outward façade of a person but at the heart – *"The Lord seeth not as man seeth; for man looketh on the outward appearance, but the Lord looketh on the heart"* 1 Samuel 16:7; 1 Chronicles 28:9.

Sin is contagious; righteousness is not – Haggai 2:11-14; 1 Corinthians 15:33.

G. Instead of being entrapped in loneliness, any person can find comfort in the peace of an intimate relationship with God. *(pages 134-135)*

___ True   ___ False

Practical:

Explain **in your own words** what each of the following verses has to do with the chapter we just read.

1. *"Ointment and perfume rejoice the heart: so doth the sweetness of a man's friend by hearty counsel"* Proverbs 27:9.

_____

_____

2. *"A true friend is always loyal, and a brother is born to help in time of need"* Proverbs 17:17 TLB.

_____

_____

For Further Study

Standing for righteousness may bring persecution, ridicule and rejection – *"Yea, and all that will live godly in Christ Jesus shall suffer persecution"* 2 Timothy 3:12. The fire you go through will purify and strengthen you – 1 Peter 1:7. Don't waste your youth and manhood giving in to peer pressure from church-wise people – Jeremiah 15:19, 20. Friendship is normal to life – *"Two are better than one…For if they fall, the one will lift up his fellow: but woe to him that is alone when he falleth; for he hath not another to help him up"* Ecclesiastes 4:9, 10. Friendship must be cultivated – *"A man that hath friends must show himself friendly"* Proverbs 18:24. The common bond of friends is their trust – *"A friend loveth at all times"* Proverbs 17:17; *"Faithful are the wounds of a friend"* Proverbs 27:6. If you find it difficult to find a friend you can trust, you can still become friends with God and ask Him to find other friends for you – Psalm 16:2, 3, 5.

3. *"These trials are only to test your faith, to see whether or not it is strong and pure. It is being tested as fire tests gold and purifies it—and your faith is far more precious to God than mere gold"* 1 Peter 1:7 TLB.

_____

_____

4. *"I don't want your sacrifices—I want your love; I don't want your offerings—I want you to know me"* Hosea 6:6 TLB.

_____

_____

Repeat this prayer out loud:

Father, in Jesus' Name, I refuse to bend or bow to low-life temptations, but I will stand strong, to the full stature of Your plan for my life. I thank You now for bringing me in to new relationships, that add to my life, not deduct from it. I choose to change today! Amen.

For Further Study

Friendship with God is based on relationship, not religion – Hosea 6:6.

How can God show Himself as a friend to us if we don't trust Him? – *"The Lord is good, a strong hold in the day of trouble; and he knoweth them that trust in him"* Nahum 1:7.

How can God befriend us if He can't trust us? – Psalm 78:57.

If we give God our all, He will enable us to overcome anything that hinders us from being His friend – 1 Corinthians 10:13.

Resolve never to give up your life because of loneliness. Always remember that God is right there to be your Friend – Hebrews 13:5, 6.

Self Test *Lesson 10*

1. Loneliness and being alone are two entirely different things. ___ True ___ False

2. Overcoming _____ is one of life's greatest feats.

3. *"Bad company corrupts good character"* 1 Corinthians 15:33 NIV.

   Read Judges 16; 1 Kings 11:1-5; 12:1-14; and 2 Chronicles 24:1, 2; 15-25. Write down some Biblical examples of people who made wrong choices because of the bad influence of companions.

   a. _____

   b. _____

   c. _____

4. What one word does every successful person have to learn to say? _____

5. What is the difference between the church-wise and the street-wise?

   _____

6. What is the only true freedom you have in life? _____

7. What holds a marriage together? _____

8. What is the common bond in all friendships? _____

9. a. Like begets _____.

   b. The common bond of rebels is their _____.

   c. Sin is _____; righteousness is _____.

Lesson 11
Write It on Your Shorts

Lesson 11
Write It on Your Shorts

A. What is the only real creative power man has? *(circle one) (page 138)*

reproduction   art   words   music

1. What three words can make you both wise and successful? *(page 139)*

   _____ _____ _____

2. What were the major differences between David and Saul? *(circle all that apply) (page 139)*

   a. Saul was taller.

   b. David loved truth.

   c. David wrote down everything God told him.

   d. Saul couldn't sing.

For Further Study
Words are powerful – *"Death and life are in the power of the tongue"* Proverbs 18:21.
There would be no Bible if men of God had not written down His revelation and truth – 2 Peter 1:20, 21;
Romans 15:4.
The Lord speaks to His children through prayer and through His Word – *"Did not our heart burn within us, while he talked with us by the way, and while he opened to us the scriptures?"* Luke 24:32. When David encountered his greatest crisis, he was able to strengthen himself by reviewing what God had done for him and His people in times past – *"And David was greatly distressed;...but David encouraged himself in the Lord his God"* 1 Samuel 30:6.
To succeed in life, you must pay careful attention to God's Word. Write down what God tells you – Proverbs 7:2, 3.
Study every word God gives you – *"I have esteemed the words of his mouth more than my necessary food"* Job 23:12.

3. Look up the following verses of Scripture and write the letter to the correct reference next to the verse. (Versions will vary, but the message will be the same.)

    a. Deuteronomy 31:19   b. Exodus 34:27   c. Proverbs 7:2, 3   d. Isaiah 8:16

    ___ *"And the Lord said to Moses, 'Write down these laws that I have given you, for they represent the terms of my covenant with you and Israel'"* TLB.

    ___ *"Now write down the words of this song, and teach it to the people of Israel as my warning to them"* TLB.

    ___ *"Obey me and live! Guard my words as your most precious possession. Write them down, and also keep them deep within your heart"* TLB.

    ___ *"Write down all these things I am going to do, says the Lord, and seal it up for the future. Entrust it to some godly man to pass on down to godly men of future generations"* TLB.

    From these passages, what appears to be important to God? _____

B. Mark "T" for True or "F" for False next to the following statements:

    ___ The core of ignorance is a poor education. *(page 140)*

    ___ A stubborn man who refuses to be taught will always be ignorant. *(page 140)*

    ___ Ignorant men will always be at the mercy of knowledgeable men. *(page 140)*

For Further Study

All discipline is based on preference – 1 Corinthians 9:25.
Discipline is the correct application of pressure – 1 Corinthians 9:27.
One of the tests of manhood is how a man handles pressure – Proverbs 24:10.
Men must be tested and proven before they can be given authority – James 1:12.
God draws lines for us and gives us boundaries for our lives so we won't be destroyed by sin – Deuteronomy 30:19.
We must discipline ourselves in order to learn – 2 Timothy 2:15.

True/False continued – Mark "T" for True or "F" for False:

___ Passing tests is a sign of learning. *(page 142)*

___ All discipline is based on good motivation and self control. *(page 143)*

___ One of the tests of manhood is how a man handles pressure. *(page 143)*

___ Discipline is the correct application of pressure. *(page 143)*

___ "You are a poor specimen if you cannot stand the stress of failure." *(page 143)*

C. Many men are trained to hear _____, not study the _____. *(page 145)*

One of the reasons men repeat mistakes is that they fail to _____. *(page 145)*

Punish in _____; reward in _____. *(page 147)*

D. Define "anarchy." *(page 148)* _____

_____

What is it a sign of? *(page 148)* _____

For Further Study

Men who read the Bible but don't apply it are spiritually ignorant – James 1:22-24.

Men repeat mistakes because they never learn from them – *"As a dog returneth to his vomit, so a fool returneth to his folly"* Proverbs 26:11.

The core of ignorance is stubbornness – *"My people are destroyed for lack of knowledge: because thou hast rejected knowledge"* Hosea 4:6.

Men fail because they have never learned how to learn – Proverbs 9:7-9; 10:8.

Decision translates into energy – *"A double minded man is unstable in all his ways"* James 1:8.

1. Define "tough love." *(page 148)* _____
   _____

   Does God like tough love? Why? *(page 148)* _____

2. "It is senseless to pay tuition to educate a rebel who has no heart for truth." *(page 150)*

   Is that statement Biblical?   ___ Yes   ___ No

   What does it mean to you? _____

3. What is the pivotal point between ruin and reconciliation? *(page 150)*

   _____   _____

E. All decisions translate into _____. *(page 150)*

   1. Name the four "D's" of success. *(pages 150-151)*

      a. _____   c. _____

      b. _____   d. _____

For Further Study

Decide to be a man of God; write down your decision – *"But as for me and my house, we will serve the Lord"* Joshua 24:15.

Decision motivates to action: Solomon – *"And Solomon determined to build an house for the name of the Lord"* 2 Chronicles 2:1.

Write down your decision, so you'll be motivated to hold to it – *"Write the vision, and make it plain upon tables, that he may run that readeth it"* Habakkuk 2:2.

It takes *dedication* to reach your goal: Jesus – Luke 9:51.

Dedication and discipline enable you to overcome all obstacles – Isaiah 50:7.

Dedicate yourself to studying and doing the Word (will) of God – *"For Ezra had prepared his heart to seek the law of the Lord, and to do it, and to teach in Israel statutes and judgments"* Ezra 7:10.

2. What is often the difference between a large company and small one? *(page 152)*

_____

3. On the paper, _____. *(page 152)*

F. The man who does the least, _____. *(page 154)*

An ounce of obedience is worth _____. *(page 156)*

For Further Study

Detail the will and plan of God for your life. Be a steward of God's words. Don't despise them by neglecting them – Isaiah 34:16.

Write down everything He tells you – Deuteronomy 6:6, 9. Write down what God has taught you today and what He teaches you day by day in the future – Revelation 1:19.

Details make the difference between success and failure – *"As the Lord commanded Moses his servant, so did Moses command Joshua, and so did Joshua; he left nothing undone of all that the Lord commanded Moses. So Joshua took all that land"* Joshua 11:15, 16.

God is concerned with detail – Matthew 10:29, 30; Psalm 139:13, 14.

The first step in attending to details is to write them down – Deuteronomy 17:18, 19.

Discipline yourself to do what God tells you to do. Give God your immediate obedience – *"I made haste, and delayed not to keep thy commandments"* Psalm 119:60.

Remember that an ounce of obedience is worth a ton of prayer – Psalm 40:6; 1 Samuel 15:22.

Practical:

Read these verses, then mark the scale below between 1 and 10 where you believe you normally are.

Proverbs 13:4   1. . . . . .5. 10
             instantly obedient   procrastinate   downright lazy

James 1:8   1. .5. 10
             focused   undecided   double-minded

Isaiah 50:7   1. .5. 10
             dedicated   off and on   don't care

Hosea 4:6   1. .5. 10
             well-educated/wise   know a few things   ignorant

What will you do this week about changing these? _____

_____

Repeat this prayer out loud:

Father, I welcome the "lines" You have placed in the "road" to guide me. I repent for any time I did not yield to them. I choose this day to be a man of decision, dedication, discipline and detail. I invite You to speak to me, and I will write it down! In Jesus' Name, Amen.

For Further Study

Laziness – Proverbs 12:24
Laziness is a sin – Romans 12:11.
Laziness brings poverty and destruction – Proverbs 10:4; 13:4; 18:9.
Procrastination is a form of laziness – Proverbs 12:11.
The man who talks most does least – Proverbs 14:23.
All a lazy man has to offer are excuses and opinions – Proverbs 26:13, 16.

Self Test   *Lesson 11*

1. David loved truth. What else was different between David and Saul?

    _____

2. What is the core of ignorance? *(circle one)*

    a. mediocrity

    b. stubbornness

    c. lack of vision

3. Ignorant men will always be at the mercy of the _____.

4. Passing exams is a sign of learning.   ___ True   ___ False

5. One of the great tests of manhood is how a man handles _____.

6. All discipline is based on _____.

7. Write down the 4 major "D's" that will determine the success or failure of a man.

    a. _____

    b. _____

    c. _____

    d. _____

8. On the paper, _____.

Lesson 12
CHAMPIONS: Men Who Never Quit

Lesson 12
CHAMPIONS: Men Who Never Quit

A. Champions are not those who never _____; they are those who never _____.
    (page 157)

   1. Use the following words to complete the sentences:

       goal   champion   born   commitment   made   winners   courage   time

       a. Fear of failure is no reason for lack of _____. *(page 157)*

       b. Failures and setbacks may occur, but the champion holds out for his _____.
           (page 157)

       c. Men love _____. *(page 157)*

       d. Champions are the right men, in the right place, at the right _____. *(page 158)*

       e. To become a champion, you must see yourself as a _____. *(page 160)*

       f. Champions are _____, not _____. *(page 160)*

       g. Champions are men in whom _____ has become visible. *(page 160)*

For Further Study
Fear of failure is no reason for lack of commitment – *"For God hath not given us the spirit of fear; but of power, and of love, and of a sound mind"* 2 Timothy 1:7.
People love winners – *"Is not this David, of whom they sang one to another in dances, saying, Saul slew his thousands, and David his ten thousands?"* 1 Samuel 29:5.
Champions are the right men, at the right place, at the right time – *"To every thing there is a season, and a time to every purpose under the heaven"* Ecclesiastes 3:1.
To become a champion, you must see yourself as a champion – *"I can do all things through Christ which strengtheneth me"* Philippians 4:13.

2. It's what you do when you are alone that determines whether you will win or lose. *(page 161)*

___ True   ___ False

3. What is the closest competition you've ever seen or been part of?

_____

What could have changed the outcome?

_____

4. Read: *"Wherefore seeing we also are compassed about with so great a cloud of witnesses, let us lay aside every weight, and the sin which doth so easily beset us, and let us run with patience the race that is set before us. Looking unto Jesus the author and finisher of our faith; who for the joy that was set before him endured the cross, despising the shame, and is set down at the right hand of the throne of God"* Hebrews 12:1-2.

Read: *"Forasmuch then as Christ hath suffered for us in the flesh, arm yourselves likewise with the same mind: for he that hath suffered in the flesh hath ceased from sin: That he no longer should live the rest of his time in the flesh to the lusts of men, but to the will of God"* 1 Peter 4:1-2.

How do these relate to the phrase "no pain, no gain"? *(page 161)*

_____

For Further Study

Champions are men in whom courage has become visible – 1 Samuel 14:6.

It is what a person does when he is alone that determines whether he will win or lose: Jesus – *"And he withdrew himself into the wilderness, and prayed"* Luke 5:16.

If you want to be a champion in life, don't waste your youth – Ecclesiastes 12:1.

There is no gain without pain – Hebrews 12:1, 2; 1 Peter 4:1, 2.

B. Give the four Hebrew words for "man" and a brief definition; then look up and read the corresponding verses. *(pages 161-162)*

1. _____ – _____ Genesis 1:26

2. _____ – _____ Genesis 2:24

3. _____ – _____ Psalm 103:15

4. _____ – _____ Psalm 37:23

C. Men who belong to God are to be members of a _____ and treat each other as such. *(page 162)*

Name three men from the Bible who were champions for God. *(pages 167-168)*

1. _____

2. _____

3. _____

For Further Study

Men who belong to God are to be members of a championship team. There are some vessels to honor, some to dishonor – 2 Timothy 2:20, 21.

We are all members of the same team – *"For whosoever shall do the will of my Father which is in heaven, the same is my brother, and sister, and mother"* Matthew 12:50.

We all train alone, but we all share the same goal God has set for us personally to attain – Philippians 3:13, 14.

Men who follow God are the right men, at the right place, at the right time – *"The steps of a good man are ordered by the Lord: and he delighteth in his way"* Psalm 37:23.

To be a true champion—a man of God—choose the more excellent way – *"Thou wilt show me the path of life: in thy presence is fulness of joy; at thy right hand there are pleasures for evermore"* Psalm 16:11.

Practical:

1. Are there failures in your life which have discouraged you from joining God's championship team? What should you do with those failures? Write it out.

   _____

   _____

   _____

2. Write out what you believe is God's opinion of you.

   _____

   _____

   _____

Principles I want to memorize:

3. Read: *"No, dear brothers, I am still not all I should be but I am bringing all my energies to bear on this one thing: Forgetting the past and looking forward to what lies ahead, I strain to reach the end of the race and receive the prize for which God is calling us up to heaven because of what Christ Jesus did for us"* Philippians 3:13-14 TLB.

    What does he do first, before looking forward?

    _____

    What does this verse inspire you to do?

    _____

Repeat this prayer out loud:

Father, in Jesus' Name, I repent for everything I've done wrong in the last few days even while I was working on this book. I want to be ready, to be the man of God You can use, to be a success, a champion, and to help minister to others Your plan for their lives. I determine to be a good steward of my time and to be first in private what I want to become in public. I know You have a plan for my life and that You are looking for me to make the decisions that will ensure me a spot on Your championship team. I will be Your man and none other's. Amen.

Self Test   *Lesson 12*

1. Champions are those who never fail.   ___ True   ___ False

2. Champions are men in whom _____ has become visible.

3. It's what you do when you are _____ that determines if you will win or lose.

4. Champions are the right men, in the right place, at the right _____.

5. Men are born champions.   ___ True   ___ False

6. Which of the four Hebrew words for man depicts man as a hero? _____ _____

7. Name the man who was the right man, at the right time, in the right place, who was used of God to release the Apostle Paul into his ministry.

    _____

8. A young man has a dream of becoming an Olympic champion in track and field. After training for an entire year, he doesn't win any races, so he quits and gives up his dream. Knowledge of what principle would have helped him?

    _____

    _____

Final Exam   COURAGE

1. The Pattern for Ministry includes:

   a. Sanctify _____ _____.   d. Use the _____ but don't touch the _____.

   b. Preach the _____.   e. Pray this _____.

   c. _____ doubting nothing.

2. Pornographers try to reach: *(circle one)*

   a. children   b. porn addicts   c. adult men

3. If young men don't see themselves as men, they won't do what?

   _____

4. Young men need to wait a few years before they can hear from God.   ___ True   ___ False

5. What are some advantages of youth?

   a. _____   c. _____

   b. _____

6. Men are to function in two roles: _____ and _____.

7. There is a difference between being a _____ and a _____.

8. In the "great commission," Jesus told us to make _____, which means to

   _____.

9. Can a young man's life be a pattern even for an older man?   ___ Yes   ___ No

10. What is the "Saul Syndrome"? _____

    _____

11. In the Bible, Timothy was trained by _____.

DETACH HERE

12. The _____ of a kingdom emanate from the _____ of the king.

13. _____ begets _____.

14. What is the pivotal point between ruin and reconciliation? _____

15. What two words did the prodigal son use when he left home? _____

    What two words started the prodigal's restoration? _____

16. Define briefly the church-wise. _____

    _____

17. Name the five reasons you need courage.

    a. _____   c. _____   e. _____

    b. _____   d. _____

18. Success is NOT based on _____.

19. Name three Bible characters that had great courage when they were young.

    a. _____   b. _____   c. _____

20. You find your life by: *(circle one)*   a. getting away from people   b. leaving home   c. losing it

21. Life is composed of _____ and _____ by your _____.

22. Men tend to judge others based on what they _____ and themselves by their _____.

23. Your ego is an absolute enemy of your manhood. You must crucify it.   ___ True   ___ False

24. You succeed in life by going to your strengths, not concentrating on your weaknesses.   ___ True   ___ False

25. How can the woman be the glory of the man unless that man is _____

    _____?

26.   Absolute peace will come only through absolute: *(circle one)*

    a.   prayer   b.   victory   c.   freedom

27.   In the "substitute society," men substitute:

    a.   Wishing for _____   c.   Fantasy for _____

    b.   Respectability for _____

28.   The Bible teaches us to live a crucified life.   ___ True ___ False

29.   The reason you don't have _____ (victory) is that you settle for _____ (truce).

30.   Name three purposes for sex.

    a.   _____   c.   _____

    b.   _____

31.   God's love is _____; His promises are _____.

32.   All pornography is _____.

33.   Sin always promises to _____ and _____ but, in reality, desires only to _____ and _____.

34.   Write out a short definition of the Principle of Release. _____

    _____

35.   Who is responsible for your life? _____

36.   Christianity is not religion; it is a _____.

37.   To honor your father and your mother is the first commandment with _____.

38.   You do only two things in life: _____ and _____.

    How you _____ determines how you _____.

39. All true joy is born out of _____.

40. When personality is gone, only _____ remains.

41. What is more important than life itself? _____

42. You cannot gain by sacrifice what you lose through disobedience.   ___ True   ___ False

43. The sin of commission is far greater than the sin of omission.   ___ True   ___ False

44. Many men want authority without: *(circle one)*

     a. hard work   b. accountability   c. declaration

45. What are the six things a man is accountable for?

     a. _____   d. _____

     b. _____   e. _____

     c. _____   f. _____

46. Your personal _____ is the cornerstone of your character.

     a. wisdom   b. insight   c. integrity

47. God commits to _____, not _____.

48. What three virtues is God looking for in your manhood?

     a. _____   c. _____

     b. _____

49. Love centers in the will.   ___ True   ___ False

50. Loneliness is normal and desirable.   ___ True   ___ False

DETACH HERE

51. The power of things you yield to in life grows _____, while what you resist grows

    _____.

52. The only true freedom you have in life is the freedom to choose between _____.

53. What makes a marriage work between times of passion? _____

54. The greatness of God and Moses' friendship was not that Moses trusted God, but that _____

    _____.

55. What three words can make you both wise and successful? _____

56. Discipline is the correct application of _____.

57. What is the core of ignorance? *(circle one)*

    a. mediocrity   b. stubbornness   c. lack of vision

58. One of the great tests of manhood is how a man handles: *(circle one)*

    a. women   b. church   c. pressure

59. Many men are trained to hear _____, not study the _____.

60. Punish in _____; reward in _____.

61. Decision translates into _____.

62. On the paper, _____.

63. Champions are not those who never _____; they are those who never _____.

64. Champions are the right men, in the right place, at the right _____.

65. Champions are made, not born.   ___ True   ___ False

66.   Short essay: What is the meaning of this verse: *"Can a man take fire to his bosom and not be burned?"* Proverbs 6:27.

Include a personal example in your answer. _____

_____

_____

_____

_____

_____

_____

_____

_____

Name _____

Address _____

Address _____

Telephone a.m. _____ p.m. _____

Email Address _____

The Final Exam is required to be "commissioned." Groups that commission graduates of the MAJORING IN MEN™ course are listed on

www.EdColeLibrary.org

DETACH HERE

Basic Daily Bible Reading

Read Proverbs each morning for wisdom, Psalms each evening for courage. Make copies of this chart and keep it in your Bible to mark off as you read. If you are just starting the habit of Bible reading, be aware that longer translations or paraphrases (such as Amplified and Living) will take longer to read each day. As you start, it is okay to read only one of the chapters in Psalms each night, instead of the many listed. Mark your chart so you'll remember which ones you haven't read.

NOTE: The chronological chart following has the rest of the chapters of Psalms that are not listed here. By using both charts together, you will cover the entire book of Psalms.

Day of Month	Proverbs	Psalms	Day of Month	Proverbs	Psalms
1	1	1, 2, 4, 5, 6			
2	2	7, 8, 9	18	18	82, 83, 84, 85
3	3	10, 11, 12, 13, 14, 15	19	19	87, 88, 91, 92
4	4	16, 17, 19, 20	20	20	93, 94, 95, 97
5	5	21, 22, 23	21	21	98, 99, 100, 101, 103
6	6	24, 25, 26, 27	22	22	104, 108
7	7	28, 29, 31, 32	23	23	109, 110, 111
8	8	33, 35	24	24	112, 113, 114, 115, 117
9	9	36, 37	25	25	119:1-56
10	10	38, 39, 40	26	26	119:57-112
11	11	41, 42, 43, 45, 46	27	27	119:113-176
12	12	47, 48, 49, 50	28	28	120, 121, 122, 124, 130,
13	13	53, 55, 58, 61, 62			131, 133, 134
14	14	64, 65, 66, 67	29	29	135, 136, 138
15	15	68, 69	30	30	139, 140, 141, 143
16	16	70, 71, 73	31	31	144, 145, 146, 148, 150
17	17	75, 76, 77, 81			

Chronological Annual Bible Reading

This schedule follows the events of the Bible chronologically and can be used with any translation or paraphrase of the Bible. Each day has an average of 77 verses of Scripture. If you follow this annually, along with your Daily Bible Reading, by your third year, you will recognize where you are and what is going to happen next. By your fifth year, you will understand the Scriptural background and setting for any reference spoken of in a message or book. At that point, the Word will become more like "meat" to you and less like "milk." Once you understand the basic stories and what happens on the surface, God can reveal to you the layers of meaning beneath. So, make copies of this chart to keep in your Bible and mark off as you read. And start reading—it's the greatest adventure in life!

Some notes:

1. Some modern translations don't have verses numbered (such as The Message), so they cannot be used with this chart. Also, if you are just starting the Bible, be aware that longer translations or paraphrases (such as Amplified and Living) tend to take longer to read each day.

2. The Daily Bible Reading chart covers the Proverbs and the chapters of Psalms that are not listed here. By using both charts together, you will cover the entire books of Psalms and Proverbs along with the rest of the Bible.

3. The chronology of Scripture is obvious in some cases, educated guesswork in others. The placement of Job, for example, is purely conjecture since there is no consensus among Bible scholars as to its date or place. For the most part, however, chronological reading helps the reader, since it places stories that have duplicated information, or prophetic utterances elsewhere in Scripture, within the same reading sequence.

HOW TO READ SCRIPTURE NOTATIONS:

Book chapter: verse. (Mark 15:44 means the book of Mark, chapter 15, verse 44.)

Book chapter; chapter (Mark 15; 16; 17 means the book of Mark, chapters 15, 16, 17.)

Books continue the same until otherwise noted. (2 Kings 22; 23:1-28; Jeremiah 20 means the book of 2 Kings, chapter 22, the book of 2 Kings, chapter 23, verses 1-28; then the book of Jeremiah, chapter 20.)

DETACH HERE

1	Jan 1	Genesis 1; 2; 3
2	Jan 2	Genesis 4; 5; 6
3	Jan 3	Genesis 7; 8; 9
4	Jan 4	Genesis 10; 11; 12
5	Jan 5	Genesis 13; 14; 15; 16
6	Jan 6	Genesis 17; 18; 19:1-29
7	Jan 7	Genesis 19:30-38; 20; 21
8	Jan 8	Genesis 22; 23; 24:1-31
9	Jan 9	Genesis 24:32-67; 25
10	Jan 10	Genesis 26; 27
11	Jan 11	Genesis 28; 29; 30:1-24
12	Jan 12	Genesis 30:25-43; 31
13	Jan 13	Genesis 32; 33; 34
14	Jan 14	Genesis 35; 36
15	Jan 15	Genesis 37; 38; 39
16	Jan 16	Genesis 40; 41
17	Jan 17	Genesis 42; 43
18	Jan 18	Genesis 44; 45
19	Jan 19	Genesis 46; 47; 48
20	Jan 20	Genesis 49; 50; Exodus 1
21	Jan 21	Exodus 2; 3; 4
22	Jan 22	Exodus 5; 6; 7
23	Jan 23	Exodus 8; 9
24	Jan 24	Exodus 10; 11; 12
25	Jan 25	Exodus 13; 14; 15
26	Jan 26	Exodus 16; 17; 18
27	Jan 27	Exodus 19; 20; 21
28	Jan 28	Exodus 22; 23; 24
29	Jan 29	Exodus 25; 26
30	Jan 30	Exodus 27; 28; 29:1-28
31	Jan 31	Exodus 29:29-46; 30; 31
32	Feb 1	Exodus 32; 33; 34
33	Feb 2	Exodus 35; 36
34	Feb 3	Exodus 37; 38
35	Feb 4	Exodus 39; 40
36	Feb 5	Leviticus 1; 2; 3; 4
37	Feb 6	Leviticus 5; 6; 7
38	Feb 7	Leviticus 8; 9; 10
39	Feb 8	Leviticus 11; 12; 13:1-37
40	Feb 9	Leviticus 13:38-59; 14
41	Feb 10	Leviticus 15; 16
42	Feb 11	Leviticus 17; 18; 19
43	Feb 12	Leviticus 20; 21; 22:1-16
44	Feb 13	Leviticus 22:17-33; 23
45	Feb 14	Leviticus 24; 25
46	Feb 15	Leviticus 26; 27
47	Feb 16	Numbers 1; 2
48	Feb 17	Numbers 3; 4:1-20
49	Feb 18	Numbers 4:21-49; 5; 6
50	Feb 19	Numbers 7
51	Feb 20	Numbers 8; 9; 10
52	Feb 21	Numbers 11; 12; 13
53	Feb 22	Numbers 14; 15
54	Feb 23	Numbers 16; 17
55	Feb 24	Numbers 18; 19; 20
56	Feb 25	Numbers 21; 22
57	Feb 26	Numbers 23; 24; 25
58	Feb 27	Numbers 26; 27
59	Feb 28	Numbers 28; 29; 30
60	Mar 1	Numbers 31; 32:1-27
61	Mar 2	Numbers 32:28-42; 33
62	Mar 3	Numbers 34; 35; 36
63	Mar 4	Deuteronomy 1; 2
64	Mar 5	Deuteronomy 3; 4
65	Mar 6	Deuteronomy 5; 6; 7
66	Mar 7	Deuteronomy 8; 9; 10
67	Mar 8	Deuteronomy 11; 12; 13
68	Mar 9	Deuteronomy 14; 15; 16
69	Mar 10	Deuteronomy 17; 18; 19; 20
70	Mar 11	Deuteronomy 21; 22; 23
71	Mar 12	Deuteronomy 24; 25; 26; 27
72	Mar 13	Deuteronomy 28
73	Mar 14	Deuteronomy 29; 30; 31
74	Mar 15	Deuteronomy 32; 33
75	Mar 16	Deuteronomy 34; Psalm 90; Joshua 1; 2
76	Mar 17	Joshua 3; 4; 5; 6
77	Mar 18	Joshua 7; 8; 9
78	Mar 19	Joshua 10; 11
79	Mar 20	Joshua 12; 13; 14
80	Mar 21	Joshua 15; 16
81	Mar 22	Joshua 17; 18; 19:1-23
82	Mar 23	Joshua 19:24-51; 20; 21
83	Mar 24	Joshua 22; 23; 24
84	Mar 25	Judges 1; 2; 3:1-11
85	Mar 26	Judges 3:12-31; 4; 5
86	Mar 27	Judges 6; 7
87	Mar 28	Judges 8; 9
88	Mar 29	Judges 10; 11; 12
89	Mar 30	Judges 13; 14; 15
90	Mar 31	Judges 16; 17; 18
91	Apr 1	Judges 19; 20
		[You have completed 1/4 of the Bible!]
92	Apr 2	Judges 21; Job 1; 2; 3
93	Apr 3	Job 4; 5; 6
94	Apr 4	Job 7; 8; 9
95	Apr 5	Job 10; 11; 12
96	Apr 6	Job 13; 14; 15
97	Apr 7	Job 16; 17; 18; 19
98	Apr 8	Job 20; 21
99	Apr 9	Job 22; 23; 24
100	Apr 10	Job 25; 26; 27; 28
101	Apr 11	Job 29; 30; 31
102	Apr 12	Job 32; 33; 34
103	Apr 13	Job 35; 36; 37
104	Apr 14	Job 38; 39
105	Apr 15	Job 40; 41; 42
106	Apr 16	Ruth 1; 2; 3
107	Apr 17	Ruth 4; 1 Samuel 1; 2
108	Apr 18	1 Samuel 3; 4; 5; 6
109	Apr 19	1 Samuel 7; 8; 9
110	Apr 20	1 Samuel 10; 11; 12; 13
111	Apr 21	1 Samuel 14; 15
112	Apr 22	1 Samuel 16; 17
113	Apr 23	1 Samuel 18; 19; Psalm 59
114	Apr 24	1 Samuel 20; 21; Psalms 34; 56
115	Apr 25	1 Samuel 22; 23; Psalms 52; 142
116	Apr 26	1 Samuel 24; 25; 1 Chronicles 12:8-18; Psalm 57
117	Apr 27	1 Samuel 26; 27; 28; Psalms 54; 63
118	Apr 28	1 Samuel 29; 30; 31; 1 Chronicles 12:1-7; 12:19-22
119	Apr 29	1 Chronicles 10; 2 Samuel 1; 2
120	Apr 30	2 Samuel 3; 4; 1 Chronicles 11:1-9; 12:23-40
121	May 1	2 Samuel 5; 6; 1 Chronicles 13; 14
122	May 2	2 Samuel 22; 1 Chronicles 15
123	May 3	1 Chronicles 16; Psalm 18
124	May 4	2 Samuel 7; Psalms 96; 105
125	May 5	1 Chronicles 17; 2 Samuel 8; 9; 10
126	May 6	1 Chronicles 18; 19; Psalm 60; 2 Samuel 11
127	May 7	2 Samuel 12; 13; 1 Chronicles 20:1-3; Psalm 51
128	May 8	2 Samuel 14; 15
129	May 9	2 Samuel 16; 17; 18; Psalm 3
130	May 10	2 Samuel 19; 20; 21
131	May 11	2 Samuel 23:8-23
132	May 12	1 Chronicles 20:4-8; 11:10-25; 2 Samuel 23:24-39; 24
133	May 13	1 Chronicles 11:26-47; 21; 22
134	May 14	1 Chronicles 23; 24; Psalm 30
135	May 15	1 Chronicles 25; 26
136	May 16	1 Chronicles 27; 28; 29
137	May 17	1 Kings 1; 2:1-12; 2 Samuel 23:1-7
138	May 18	1 Kings 2:13-46; 3; 2 Chronicles 1:1-13
139	May 19	1 Kings 5; 6; 2 Chronicles 2
140	May 20	1 Kings 7; 2 Chronicles 3; 4
141	May 21	1 Kings 8; 2 Chronicles 5
142	May 22	1 Kings 9; 2 Chronicles 6; 7:1-10
143	May 23	1 Kings 10:1-13; 2 Chronicles 7:11-22; 8; 9:1-12; 1 Kings 4
144	May 24	1 Kings 10:14-29; 2 Chronicles 1:14-17; 9:13-28; Psalms 72; 127
145	May 25	Song of Solomon 1; 2; 3; 4; 5
146	May 26	Song of Solomon 6; 7; 8; 1 Kings 11:1-40
147	May 27	Ecclesiastes 1; 2; 3; 4
148	May 28	Ecclesiastes 5; 6; 7; 8
149	May 29	Ecclesiastes 9; 10; 11; 12; 1 Kings 11:41-43; 2 Chronicles 9:29-31
150	May 30	1 Kings 12; 2 Chronicles 10; 11
151	May 31	1 Kings 13; 14; 2 Chronicles 12
152	June 1	1 Kings 15; 2 Chronicles 13; 14; 15
153	June 2	1 Kings 16; 2 Chronicles 16; 17
154	June 3	1 Kings 17; 18; 19
155	June 4	1 Kings 20; 21
156	June 5	1 Kings 22; 2 Chronicles 18
157	June 6	2 Kings 1; 2; 2 Chronicles 19; 20; 21:1-3
158	June 7	2 Kings 3; 4
159	June 8	2 Kings 5; 6; 7
160	June 9	2 Kings 8; 9; 2 Chronicles 21:4-20
161	June 10	2 Chronicles 22; 23; 2 Kings 10; 11
162	June 11	Joel 1; 2; 3
163	June 12	2 Kings 12; 13; 2 Chronicles 24
164	June 13	2 Kings 14; 2 Chronicles 25; Jonah 1
165	June 14	Jonah 2; 3; 4; Hosea 1; 2; 3; 4
166	June 15	Hosea 5; 6; 7; 8; 9; 10
167	June 16	Hosea 11; 12; 13; 14

DETACH HERE

168	June 17	2 Kings 15:1-7; 2 Chronicles 26; Amos 1; 2; 3
169	June 18	Amos 4; 5; 6; 7
170	June 19	Amos 8; 9; 2 Kings 15:8-18; Isaiah 1
171	June 20	Isaiah 2; 3; 4; 2 Kings 15:19-38; 2 Chronicles 27
172	June 21	Isaiah 5; 6; Micah 1; 2; 3
173	June 22	Micah 4; 5; 6; 7; 2 Kings 16:1-18
174	June 23	2 Chronicles 28; Isaiah 7; 8
175	June 24	Isaiah 9; 10; 11; 12
176	June 25	Isaiah 13; 14; 15; 16
177	June 26	Isaiah 17; 18; 19; 20; 21
178	June 27	Isaiah 22; 23; 24; 25
179	June 28	Isaiah 26; 27; 28; 29
180	June 29	Isaiah 30; 31; 32; 33
181	June 30	Isaiah 34; 35; 2 Kings 18:1-8; 2 Chronicles 29
182	July 1	2 Chronicles 30; 31; 2 Kings 17; 2 Kings 16:19-20

[You have completed 1/2 of the Bible!]

183	July 2	2 Kings 18:9-37; 2 Chronicles 32:1-19; Isaiah 36
184	July 3	2 Kings 19; 2 Chronicles 32:20-23; Isaiah 37
185	July 4	2 Kings 20; 21:1-18; 2 Chronicles 32:24-33; Isaiah 38; 39
186	July 5	2 Chronicles 33:1-20; Isaiah 40; 41
187	July 6	Isaiah 42; 43; 44
188	July 7	Isaiah 45; 46; 47; 48
189	July 8	Isaiah 49; 50; 51; 52
190	July 9	Isaiah 53; 54; 55; 56; 57
191	July 10	Isaiah 58; 59; 60; 61; 62
192	July 11	Isaiah 63; 64; 65; 66
193	July 12	2 Kings 21:19-26; 2 Chronicles 33:21-25; 34:1-7; Zephaniah 1; 2; 3
194	July 13	Jeremiah 1; 2; 3
195	July 14	Jeremiah 4; 5
196	July 15	Jeremiah 6; 7; 8
197	July 16	Jeremiah 9; 10; 11
198	July 17	Jeremiah 12; 13; 14; 15
199	July 18	Jeremiah 16; 17; 18; 19
200	July 19	Jeremiah 20; 2 Kings 22; 23:1-28
201	July 20	2 Chronicles 34:8-33; 35:1-19; Nahum 1; 2; 3
202	July 21	2 Kings 23:29-37; 2 Chronicles 35:20-27; 36:1-5; Jeremiah 22:10-17; 26; Habakkuk 1
203	July 22	Habakkuk 2; 3; Jeremiah 46; 47; 2 Kings 24:1-4; 2 Chronicles 36:6-7
204	July 23	Jeremiah 25; 35; 36; 45
205	July 24	Jeremiah 48; 49:1-33
206	July 25	Daniel 1; 2
207	July 26	Jeremiah 22:18-30; 2 Kings 24:5-20; 2 Chronicles 36:8-12; Jeremiah 37:1-2; 52:1-3; 24; 29
208	July 27	Jeremiah 27; 28; 23
209	July 28	Jeremiah 50; 51:1-19
210	July 29	Jeremiah 51:20-64; 49:34-39; 34
211	July 30	Ezekiel 1; 2; 3; 4
212	July 31	Ezekiel 5; 6; 7; 8
213	Aug 1	Ezekiel 9; 10; 11; 12
214	Aug 2	Ezekiel 13, 14, 15, 16:1-34
215	Aug 3	Ezekiel 16:35-63; 17; 18
216	Aug 4	Ezekiel 19; 20
217	Aug 5	Ezekiel 21; 22
218	Aug 6	Ezekiel 23; 2 Kings 25:1; 2 Chronicles 36:13-16; Jeremiah 39:1; 52:4; Ezekiel 24
219	Aug 7	Jeremiah 21; 22:1-9; 32; 30
220	Aug 8	Jeremiah 31; 33; Ezekiel 25
221	Aug 9	Ezekiel 29:1-16; 30; 31; 26
222	Aug 10	Ezekiel 27; 28; Jeremiah 37:3-21
223	Aug 11	Jeremiah 38; 39:2-10; 52:5-30
224	Aug 12	2 Kings 25:2-22; 2 Chronicles 36:17-21; Jeremiah 39:11-18; 40:1-6; Lamentations 1
225	Aug 13	Lamentations 2; 3
226	Aug 14	Lamentations 4; 5; Obadiah; Jeremiah 40:7-16
227	Aug 15	Jeremiah 41; 42; 43; 44; 2 Kings 25:23-26
228	Aug 16	Ezekiel 33:21-33; 34; 35; 36
229	Aug 17	Ezekiel 37; 38; 39
230	Aug 18	Ezekiel 32; 33:1-20; Daniel 3
231	Aug 19	Ezekiel 40; 41
232	Aug 20	Ezekiel 42; 43; 44
233	Aug 21	Ezekiel 45; 46; 47
234	Aug 22	Ezekiel 48; 29:17-21; Daniel 4
235	Aug 23	Jeremiah 52:31-34; 2 Kings 25:27-30; Psalms 44; 74; 79
236	Aug 24	Psalms 80; 86; 89
237	Aug 25	Psalms 102; 106
238	Aug 26	Psalms 123; 137; Daniel 7; 8
239	Aug 27	Daniel 5; 9; 6
240	Aug 28	2 Chronicles 36:22-23; Ezra 1; 2
241	Aug 29	Ezra 3; 4:1-5; Daniel 10; 11
242	Aug 30	Daniel 12; Ezra 4:6-24; 5; 6:1-13; Haggai 1
243	Aug 31	Haggai 2; Zechariah 1; 2; 3
244	Sept 1	Zechariah 4; 5; 6; 7; 8
245	Sept 2	Ezra 6:14-22; Psalm 78
246	Sept 3	Psalms 107; 116; 118
247	Sept 4	Psalms 125; 126; 128; 129; 132; 147
248	Sept 5	Psalm 149; Zechariah 9; 10; 11; 12; 13
249	Sept 6	Zechariah 14; Esther 1; 2; 3
250	Sept 7	Esther 4; 5; 6; 7; 8
251	Sept 8	Esther 9; 10; Ezra 7; 8
252	Sept 9	Ezra 9; 10; Nehemiah 1
253	Sept 10	Nehemiah 2; 3; 4; 5
254	Sept 11	Nehemiah 6; 7
255	Sept 12	Nehemiah 8; 9; 10
256	Sept 13	Nehemiah 11; 12
257	Sept 14	Nehemiah 13; Malachi 1; 2; 3; 4
258	Sept 15	1 Chronicles 1; 2:1-35
259	Sept 16	1 Chronicles 2:36-55; 3; 4
260	Sept 17	1 Chronicles 5; 6:1-41
261	Sept 18	1 Chronicles 6:42-81; 7
262	Sept 19	1 Chronicles 8; 9
263	Sept 20	Matthew 1; 2; 3; 4
264	Sept 21	Matthew 5; 6
265	Sept 22	Matthew 7; 8
266	Sept 23	Matthew 9; 10
267	Sept 24	Matthew 11; 12
268	Sept 25	Matthew 13; 14
269	Sept 26	Matthew 15; 16
270	Sept 27	Matthew 17; 18; 19
271	Sept 28	Matthew 20; 21
272	Sept 29	Matthew 22; 23
273	Sept 30	Matthew 24; 25

[You have completed 3/4 of the Bible!]

274	Oct 1	Matthew 26; 27; 28
275	Oct 2	Mark 1; 2
276	Oct 3	Mark 3; 4
277	Oct 4	Mark 5; 6
278	Oct 5	Mark 7; 8:1-26
279	Oct 6	Mark 8:27-38; 9
280	Oct 7	Mark 10; 11
281	Oct 8	Mark 12; 13
282	Oct 9	Mark 14
283	Oct 10	Mark 15; 16
284	Oct 11	Luke 1
285	Oct 12	Luke 2; 3
286	Oct 13	Luke 4; 5
287	Oct 14	Luke 6; 7:1-23
288	Oct 15	Luke 7:24-50; 8
289	Oct 16	Luke 9
290	Oct 17	Luke 10; 11
291	Oct 18	Luke 12; 13
292	Oct 19	Luke 14; 15
293	Oct 20	Luke 16; 17
294	Oct 21	Luke 18; 19
295	Oct 22	Luke 20; 21
296	Oct 23	Luke 22
297	Oct 24	Luke 23; 24:1-28
298	Oct 25	Luke 24:29-53; John 1
299	Oct 26	John 2; 3; 4:1-23
300	Oct 27	John 4:24-54; 5; 6:1-7
301	Oct 28	John 6:8-71; 7:1-21
302	Oct 29	John 7:22-53; 8
303	Oct 30	John 9; 10
304	Oct 31	John 11; 12:1-28
305	Nov 1	John 12:29-50; 13; 14
306	Nov 2	John 15; 16; 17
307	Nov 3	John 18; 19:1-24
308	Nov 4	John 19:25-42; 20; 21
309	Nov 5	Acts 1; 2
310	Nov 6	Acts 3; 4
311	Nov 7	Acts 5; 6
312	Nov 8	Acts 7
313	Nov 9	Acts 8; 9
314	Nov 10	Acts 10
315	Nov 11	Acts 11
316	Nov 12	Acts 12; 13
317	Nov 13	Acts 14; 15; Galatians 1
318	Nov 14	Galatians 2; 3; 4
319	Nov 15	Galatians 5; 6; James 1
320	Nov 16	James 2; 3; 4; 5
321	Nov 17	Acts 16; 17
322	Nov 18	Acts 18:1-11; 1 Thessalonians 1; 2; 3; 4

323	Nov 19	1 Thessalonians 5;
		2 Thessalonians 1; 2; 3
324	Nov 20	Acts 18:12-28; 19:1-22;
		1 Corinthians 1
325	Nov 21	1 Corinthians 2; 3; 4; 5
326	Nov 22	1 Corinthians 6; 7; 8
327	Nov 23	1 Corinthians 9; 10; 11
328	Nov 24	1 Corinthians 12; 13; 14
329	Nov 25	1 Corinthians 15; 16
330	Nov 26	Acts 19:23-41; 20:1;
		2 Corinthians 1; 2
331	Nov 27	2 Corinthians 3; 4; 5
332	Nov 28	2 Corinthians 6; 7; 8; 9
333	Nov 29	2 Corinthians 10; 11; 12
334	Nov 30	2 Corinthians 13; Romans 1; 2
335	Dec 1	Romans 3; 4; 5
336	Dec 2	Romans 6; 7; 8
337	Dec 3	Romans 9; 10; 11

338	Dec 4	Romans 12; 13; 14
339	Dec 5	Romans 15; 16
340	Dec 6	Acts 20:2-38; 21
341	Dec 7	Acts 22; 23
342	Dec 8	Acts 24; 25; 26
343	Dec 9	Acts 27; 28
344	Dec 10	Ephesians 1; 2; 3
345	Dec 11	Ephesians 4; 5; 6
346	Dec 12	Colossians 1; 2; 3
347	Dec 13	Colossians 4; Philippians 1; 2
348	Dec 14	Philippians 3; 4; Philemon
349	Dec 15	1 Timothy 1; 2; 3; 4
350	Dec 16	1 Timothy 5; 6; Titus 1; 2
351	Dec 17	Titus 3; 2 Timothy 1; 2; 3
352	Dec 18	2 Timothy 4; 1 Peter 1; 2
353	Dec 19	1 Peter 3; 4; 5; Jude
354	Dec 20	2 Peter 1; 2; 3; Hebrews 1
355	Dec 21	Hebrews 2; 3; 4; 5

356	Dec 22	Hebrews 6; 7; 8; 9
357	Dec 23	Hebrews 10; 11
358	Dec 24	Hebrews 12; 13; 2 John; 3 John
359	Dec 25	1 John 1; 2; 3; 4
360	Dec 26	1 John 5; Revelation 1; 2
361	Dec 27	Revelation 3; 4; 5; 6
362	Dec 28	Revelation 7; 8; 9; 10; 11
363	Dec 29	Revelation 12; 13; 14; 15
364	Dec 30	Revelation 16; 17; 18; 19
365	Dec 31	Revelation 20; 21; 22

You have completed the entire Bible-Congratulations!

DETACH HERE

NANCY CORBETT COLE CHARITIES

A portion of the proceeds from this book will be given to Nancy Corbett Cole Charities, serving the abused, addicted and abandoned. Internationally, "Nancy Corbett Cole Homes of Refuge" provide housing, vocational training and education for abused women and children. In the United States, help is ongoing on an individual and corporate basis.

Nancy Corbett Cole, "The Loveliest Lady in the Land," supported her husband, Edwin Louis Cole, in pursuing his life's mission for 54 years. Behind the scenes, she was a spiritual anchor and provider for many. Before her death in December 2000, Nancy asked for the assurance that those for whom she had provided would not feel her absence. To fulfill that end, and for that purpose, Nancy Corbett Cole Charities were established.

By purchasing this book, you have helped society's under-served and less privileged members. If this book helped you, please consider sending a generous donation as well. Your one-time or continual support will help the helpless, heal the hurting and relieve the needy. Your gift is fully tax-deductible in the U.S. Send your compassionate contribution to:

Nancy Corbett Cole Charities
P. O. Box 92501
Southlake, TX 76092
USA
Thank you for your cheerful and unselfish care for others.

Watch for more Watercolor Books®

by terrific authors like –

Edwin Louis Cole

Nancy Corbett Cole

G. F. Watkins

Steve Riggle

Ron DePriest

Karen Davis

Many more!

Southlake, Texas

ABOUT THE AUTHOR

Edwin Louis Cole, an internationally-acclaimed speaker, best-selling author and motivational lecturer, was known for his practical application of wisdom from Kingdom principles. Through his books, tapes and videos, the ministry to men continues to reach thousands of men worldwide each month with a prophetic voice, challenging them to fulfill their potential for true manhood, which is Christlikeness. His books have sold in the millions, including the landmark *Maximized Manhood*. Over five million people have studied his principles in the last fifty years. Considered "the father of the Christian men's movement," Edwin Louis Cole commissioned other men who now travel extensively worldwide to strengthen the ministry bases he founded under the divine guidance of the Holy Spirit.

Dr. Cole's lifetime body of work is being compiled at

www.EdColeLibrary.org

For more information, write:

Ed Cole® Library
P.O. Box 92921
Southlake, TX 76092

Also by Edwin Louis Cole

Maximized Manhood
The Power of Potential
Real Man
Strong Men in Tough Times
Absolute Answers to Prodigal Problems
COURAGE
Winners Are Not Those Who Never Fail but Those Who NEVER QUIT!
Communication, Sex and Money
The Unique Woman
TREASURE
Irresistible Husband
Sexual Integrity

Study curriculum available for most books.
Answer keys for MAJORING IN MEN™ curriculum can be found at
www.watercolorbooks.com

LEARN TO DISCIPLE MEN AND KEEP 70% OF YOUR CONVERTS IN YOUR CHURCH!

How do we "shut the back door" of the church and disciple the men God brings us? The G-MEN Strategy gives Christians purpose and a plan for spiritual growth, personal mentoring and evangelism. G-MEN are the *missing link* for building the Kingdom of God!

Designed and written by a pastor, these principles are flexible for any group or culture and easy to use. The G-MEN Strategy links the *problem* of discipling new converts with a *plan*. Mapped out step by step, these practical applications bring order, build the church and take the Gospel to the world. It's no theory. It's a time-tested plan of action that is world-changing revelation.

Can the G-MEN Strategy change the world? It already is!

Available in bookstores or contact www.watercolorbooks.com